COACH

COACH

*The life and soccer times
of Clive Barker*

MICHAEL MARNEWICK

JACANA

First published by Jacana Media (Pty) Ltd in 2018

10 Orange Street
Sunnyside
Auckland Park 2092
South Africa
+2711 628 3200
www.jacana.co.za

ISBN 978-1-4314-2673-7

Design by Shawn Paikin and Maggie Davey
Photographs © Gavin Barker, unless otherwise specified
Editing by Sean Fraser
Proofreading by Megan Mance
Index by Megan Mance
Set in Stempel Garamond 11/15pt
Job no. 003306

Printed by **novus print**, a Novus Holdings company

See a complete list of Jacana titles at www.jacana.co.za

To my wife, Yvonne,
in gratitude for her loyalty, support and love …
in good times and bad.
Words are not enough.

– CLIVE BARKER

Contents

Clive playing for Durban City, 1960. (Ronnie De Villiers)

ONE

Humble Beginnings

"Football has been my life, my passion."
– Clive Barker

There hasn't been a day in nearly 65 years that I haven't been involved in football or thought about the game in one way or another, be it playing or coaching. It has brought me immense satisfaction, as well as frustration, plenty of grey hair, but also much joy.

I've travelled the world, met great people, coached wonderful players and fantastic teams and, in all of this, I feel very privileged to have played some small role in the development of a sport revered by millions. South Africa was badly fractured by apartheid, but through it all, football played a significant role in unifying the nation when it needed harmony.

Some of my harshest critics believed that, as a white coach in a black-dominated sport, taking me for a foreigner, I would be out of touch and unable to grasp the complexities of South African football. It was probably my greatest frustration with the local press and a view I considered insulting. I was at pains to rectify this whenever the issue was raised. I guess the misperception was born out of the fact that it was unusual for a white South African to be involved, at a coaching level, in what was considered a black sport in the 1970s and 1980s. Even today, people are under that impression, so let me put the doubters to rest that I'm a South African through and through – born on 19 June 1944 in Bellair, a suburb of Durban, KwaZulu-Natal.

My dad, Robert Lawrence Barker, played in the midfield for the local football team – Hillary Football Club – and boxed at an amateur level, going on to represent Natal. He could also play the banjo and, together with my mother's skill on the piano, many a fine tune would be played on a Saturday night. I don't think it's any surprise or coincidence that football, boxing and music have played their part in my life.

My mother, Patricia Amelia Mary, was a dance instructor with a studio at the Sea View MOTH Hall in Bellair and when Princess Elizabeth and Princess Margaret came out to South Africa with their parents, King George VI and Queen Elizabeth, in 1947, my mom danced for them at a tea party – Mom's claim to fame. Recently, I visited a local church near my home in Glenwood, and waited until after the service to chat to the organ player, thanking him for playing so beautifully. His enthusiasm had everyone singing as if they had been accompanied by an orchestra. During our conversation, he asked if I was the football man, and I told him I was. He said that he wanted to share something with me: "I watched your mother dance to a song called 'Sleepy Lagoon', and I'll never forget how beautifully she moved." It was marvellous that this stranger was able to remember Mom dance more than 70 years ago; it filled me with immense pride.

My sister Penny was a *laatlammetjie*, but the idol of our family and my wife Yvonne had a huge influence in bringing her up. Together, my brothers Lawrie and Arthur and I would spend every afternoon in the garden kicking the ball around until the radio programme *Superman* would come on and we'd forgo our heroics for those of our superhero.

Sadly, my mom and dad both died at the tender age of 46; how I wish we could have this time again.

My recollection of growing up in Bellair is filled with happy memories ... I attended a wonderful school, Bellair Primary, and was given every opportunity to succeed. Bellair Primary was very small – I recall there being about 10 pupils in my class, but realistically there were probably more than that. When you're little, the world is a big place, but your immediate surroundings seem much smaller. This was a football-playing school; the deputy principal, Mr McMillan, was fanatical about the sport and I needed little encouragement to participate. Bellair Primary provided me with a fabulous upbringing and I'm happy to report that the school is still in existence today.

I recall one particular teacher, Mrs Hesom, writing in one of my reports: "A charming manner won't get you through life – you'll have to go out and work a lot harder."

This was my first lesson in life.

Because my mother was a dance teacher, we would put together a show each year to collect money for the MOTHs in Sea View and Bellair. It was a tradition for me to get up on stage and open the concert singing 'There's no Business like Show Business' and copy the likes of Frank Sinatra.

But my performing days lasted only as long as I was the cute kid singing on stage. Football took over in a big way and the sport consumed me completely. Every present I received would be football related.

Every Friday night I would clean my boots until they were spotless and then wash the laces, and on Saturday morning my mates and I would catch a train to Central Station in Durban. We would make our way to the football field and the Under-11s would start the day's action. It was a big thing to represent your school against the other local schools.

We would finish the game breathless but excited, hoping that someone wouldn't turn up for the Under-13 match that followed. That way, if you were good enough, the coaches might ask you to come play again; the likelihood of playing two matches in the morning was pretty high. Later, the first team would play in the league from which the Natal team was eventually selected.

My high-school days were spent at Glenwood Boys' High, which was not a soccer school – not at all – and it was a tough time for me. In fact, because of the pressure they had put on him to play rugby instead of football, my brother left Glenwood, knowing the school's sporting priorities – that rugby was for white people and football for the black population – would limit his sporting opportunities. He slipped out for Natal Schools' trials and was caught. Eventually my father removed Arthur and sent him to school in Queensburgh. I think the really negative sentiment towards football was because they were protecting rugby.

I was able to keep up my footballing by playing for the Berea Park Under-14 to Under-16 teams, but just as I was about to start playing professionally, the school informed me in no uncertain terms that I *would* be playing rugby. Norman Elliott and John Watkins from Durban City went to see Mr JB Colam, the Glenwood principal, to try to coax him into allowing me to stick with football, but without success.

Thus began a shining career in rugby that lasted all of 80 minutes. My first match was against St Henry's and my less-than-superb performance must have convinced them that my future lay with a round rather than an oval ball. I'm happy to report that I was subsequently released from rugby duty to play football for Durban City.

My academic record at high school probably mirrors my prowess on the rugby field. When I was preparing to write exams, I would move in with my grandparents because my granny looked after us so well. It didn't help me pass though – I was thicker than two short planks.

In 1960 I signed my first playing contract with Durban City. I was only 16 and because of my young age and small stature, was nicknamed the "Darling of Kingsmead".

It was a daunting experience playing at such a young age in the top league but I was determined to realise my dream of playing at that level – with the hope of one day going across to play in England.

My progress was hampered when I damaged my knee playing against Rangers in Johannesburg. I went up for a challenge and came down awkwardly, tearing ligaments in my knee.

In those days there were no quick fix operations for ligament damage like there are today and it took time for the injury to heal. However, even without regular game time in my first season, the local fans and media took a liking to me, describing me as: "A left-sided half back with an educated left foot."

At the end of the season it was expected that I would renew my contract but Durban United came in with a signing-on fee that I could not refuse and I joined City's biggest rival.

The move made headlines and I was not sure I had done the right thing as City had taken a chance on me a year earlier, but I believed it was the best move for my career at the time.

The English clubs that were touring here then were also showing an interest and I was invited by both Leicester and Tottenham Hotspur to train with them while the teams were in the country.

There was huge media speculation that I would be invited for a trial with Leicester when they returned to the United Kingdom, but the knee injury flared up again and I missed the opportunity.

There has always been a good balance in my life and it was during a stint on the sidelines that I met Yvonne. Perhaps my family life and ultimately my coaching career might have been very different if I had continued with my playing career.

When I was 24 I damaged my other knee and realised that my playing days were sadly behind me; I retired to concentrate on other things.

Although my career was not spectacular and was cut short due to my injuries, those eight years of playing experience would prove crucial in shaping my coaching career.

At that time, football was on its way up; school football was well structured, with many young players aspiring to play at club level. Professional football was the next step and, if you were good enough and lucky enough, you were chosen to play for Durban City, or the opposition, Durban United. This boded well for professional football, but the real tragedy was that black people were not allowed to watch or participate in these games.

The stadiums would be filled and teams were able to draw crowds upward of 30 000 – but there would be only white sides playing. In the background, questions were being asked: "Why only white people?"

In opposition to this league was the Federation, a breakaway group determined to create a non-racial football structure. The organisation was fairly radical and made up of lawyers and top businessmen who refused to accept normal football in an abnormal society. We aspired to play in and against the Federation teams, but our league had not crossed over into non-racialism. We knew that if we were to be part of the Federation, we'd attract quality players and many more supporters – of all races.

Professional football was growing and there was always going to come a turning point. Being kicked out of the FIFA – the International Federation of Association Football – and not being able to play anyone else in the world, including the touring FA Cup-winning teams, was the sporting world's answer to bring to an end the terrible apartheid system.

But it was still exciting to see an amateur side selected from Natal – sadly, an all-white side – to play against the likes of Newcastle United, Bolton Wanderers and Preston North End, who would come out to South Africa on a regular basis at the end of the season and try to give us a spanking. For all our efforts to beat them, nine times out of 10, they won. The better part of nine Springboks came out of Durban City in those matches in the early 1960s.

After leaving school, I spent nine months in the army before working at Kings Sports and then Swift Industrials. I then decided to go into business for myself, which turned out to be an absolute nightmare. I was utterly hopeless and it all went pear-shaped very quickly.

Denny Taylor and I had been reps for Bosch car batteries and decided we would go out together as agents; unfortunately, things didn't pan out the way we hoped they might and I ended up going into liquidation. I was left with the choice of either losing our house or trying to find ways to pay back what I owed and made an offer to pay back 100 cents in the rand.

One of the footballers I was coaching at the time, who was studying for an accounting degree, said to me, "Don't be a fool. Why are you offering them 100c? Make an offer of compromise, say 60c to the rand, and let them at least recoup the value of the items at cost." I explained that I didn't want to have to cross the road to avoid people I owed money to and he said that if that was my choice, then fine, but people would be happy to accept less, as long as there was some offer that would at least cover the cost of the article and they could avoid losing money. I paid every cent back, but it took a couple of years to do it.

In order to settle my debts, I'd work during the day for Oldhams, also in the battery game, then park my car in the garage after work and drive taxis in the evenings. Being a taxi driver was never looked down upon and it was a job I enjoyed. I'd finish ferrying people around the shows, restaurants and nightclubs at about 1am, come back home to sleep, before Yvonne would wake me at 7:30am so I could get to work at 8am and start all over again.

I had known Barry Richards since high school. He was a year younger, though, and attended the wrong school. Durban High School, commonly known as DHS, was then – and remains – a huge rival of Glenwood. The two of us met as adversaries on the cricket pitch, a true pleasure for me. I have always felt that he and Graeme Pollock were the finest batsmen South Africa ever produced. I certainly believed it when I watched the two of them scoring 103 runs in an hour after lunch against Australia in 1970. It was incredible.

When I next bumped into Barry, I was driving people around in my taxi and he was playing for Natal. He had featured against Transvaal at the Wanderers in a tense match that had us batting into a situation where he may have saved the game, but went on the hook, miscued the shot and was out for about 140.

One evening, a couple of days later, I pulled up outside Cookie Look at the Claridges Hotel on the Durban beachfront and there was Barry. He looked at me and asked: "Hey, Barks, what are you doing driving taxis?" Cheekily, I responded, "Hey, Barry, what are you doing hooking the ball and getting caught on the boundary when you could have won the game for us?"

Driving a taxi was an honest living, though, and I had debt to repay. Tips always helped and the biggest I ever received was from a postman. I had given his party a lift from Addington Beach to where the *Isle of Capri* was berthed for a fishing expedition. Soon after I dropped them off, I received a message from dispatch, instructing me to return to fetch the postman and his friend. When I arrived, he told me that the captain of the boat was unlikely to search too hard for the fish unless he was put in a suitably happy mood. This necessitated a speedy trip to Umgeni Road where the postman rushed into an unofficial liquor store to buy the captain some liquid refreshment at an outrageous price. But he was clearly so impressed with my service that he tipped me R5.

Saturdays and Sundays were the busiest, when we would make the most money, and I have fond memories of my stint driving taxis and of some fantastic people. It may have been an incredibly tough six months, but it was a wonderful time in my life.

But my financial woes were not quite over. One afternoon Yvonne called me to say that our furniture had been removed and suggested in no uncertain terms that if I wanted anything to eat or drink that evening, as well as somewhere to sit, I needed to make sure I went and got it all back. Rather than face the wrath of my wife, I went and picked it all up right away.

By then I had come to realise that there had to be an easier way to make money and decided to start coaching football. My introduction was coaching the amateur side St Patrick's near the Coedmore Quarries. Together with Father Boardman and Lionel Williams from Durban City (the latter one of the best players to have represented South Africa) we – they, more than myself – decided to help out. The area had its share of problems and we felt that if we could get the kids onto the football fields, it would keep them out of mischief.

When I started, I couldn't afford the balls and equipment required, and so, fairly deviously I must admit, I watched as parents dropped their children off at school and would then, in my most charming way, mercilessly harass those driving the best cars to get them to assist with buying a football or two.

It was a wonderful start to my coaching career and we had a few very talented players there, but I decided that I needed to get paid – and then the coaching job at Fynnlands came up.

Fynnlands was my first coaching job at an amateur club and it proved an absolute disaster. I worked them really hard; in those days, you only ever trained on Tuesdays and Thursdays and then played on the weekend, but I tormented that team. We added a Friday training session in which we focused on dead-ball situations, an area that wasn't my strength. But the harder I trained them, the worse they performed and we were relegated. A terrible start for any football coach, but perhaps a good lesson to learn because the following year we were able to take the foot off the pedal, were more sensible with our approach, more relaxed, and went on to win the league and make our way back into the top amateur league again.

A lot of people felt that the skill levels of amateur football weren't as high as the professional league, but the amateurs were the feeder players into pro teams such as Durban City and Durban United. The Durban City team that won the Pro league twice (in 1981 and 1982) and came third the following year was successful precisely because of the strength of the local amateur league.

I remember Durban City's chairman Norman Elliott asking, "Why is it necessary for Durban City to have a nursery when the whole of KZN is my nursery?" He was completely right.

I stayed with Fynnlands for a couple of years, right up until the start of the first football tournament that featured sides from all the race groups, including a side named the Continentals, made up of Lebanese, Greek and Portuguese players.

The Benson & Hedges Tournament was an exciting and ground-breaking competition, and also the first time that white teams played against black teams. Held in 1974 and also known as the Embassy

Multinational Series, I was given the role of coaching the Indian team and I truly loved my time spent with these great players. Our first game was against the black side, in Cape Town, and although my team wasn't exceptionally talented, I tried to get them super fit because I felt that this would be our only hope.

I believed we could be really competitive if we were fitter than our opposition and if we could get into the faces of our opponents, we could make it as difficult as possible for them. We trained at Hartleyvale, and the next thing a group of reporters and photographers started running towards us. I thought to myself, Wow, I can't believe we've made such a stir in Cape Town, but they ran right past us, towards a huge luxury bus that had pulled in behind us carrying the black team, featuring the likes of Shakes Mashaba, Sugar Ray Xulu, Jomo Sono – legendary players – and everyone made a beeline towards them. We realised how up against it we were.

Jacob Meer was the chairman of my side and he doubled as team selector, making sure that every player who was picked had some connection to a father, uncle or cousin he had played with. Although there was more than a hint of favouritism, the team nevertheless performed with distinction.

Our training regime was tough. After each morning session, I would make the players run a couple of kilometres up a hill where they would have lunch and I'd give them a few hours off. Then I'd make them run back down the hill. At the end of the day's second training session, I'd make them run back up the hill again.

And so they got fitter and fitter, better and better, and with that, their confidence grew. I remember looking at the clock with a few minutes to go, with the South African Black XI leading 3–2. We were on top of them and the black side were just hanging on. If we had won that match, the white team would have taken the tournament. We hung on, played good-quality football and it was incredible to have 40 000 people supporting us. Every time we touched the ball, everyone cheered us on. We ran them close.

But to hear the crowds … The only other time I ever felt that passion was the dawn of democracy when Nelson Mandela was released after 27 years in prison.

Then, in the final match between the black and white teams, played at the Rand Stadium, things turned sour.

There was an incredible amount of hype and emotion because for the first time it was black players versus white players. It was a supercharged evening. During the game against the white team, coached by Roy Bailey, the black team's Chilean coach Mario Tuani objected to a decision on an offside goal against his team. He thought that racial bias had come into the referee's decision.

The half-time break came, and in those days it was 10 minutes long, but 10 minutes became 15, then 20, and still the black team hadn't emerged from the changing rooms.

Because of the importance of the occasion – no one wanted anything to go wrong – this was a tense situation and Les Salton, who was sitting next to me, remarked what an inordinately long break this was.

We then discovered that the door to the black changing room had been locked – with them inside. Mario had refused to let them out, claiming that his team wasn't getting a fair chance; in those days, the calls went the way of the team with the most vocal support.

It was like a pressure cooker and the last thing we needed was for football to be set back even further. But sanity prevailed; the game did continue and the white side went on to beat the black side 2–0 that day, with the Continentals, ably coached by Kai Johansen, winning the overall tournament.

Mario was never given another team in the tournament to manage.

Aside from the final, we had a wonderful time because the Indian side was under no pressure. No one expected us to do well, and yet the players played above themselves. In our curtain-raiser to the final that evening, we had a couple of good players who really turned it on.

When it seemed that amateur football was going through a tough time, in competition with the professional leagues, players from the local clubs in Durban got together and decided to form a breakaway team called Durban Chiefs – one, as it turns out, that never lost a single game. This multiracial team broke down a number of barriers and, boy, could they play. We called the good players and they came. We had decided we were going into the black market and in our first game we received the grand match fee of a pie and Coke.

One game was played against Enseleni in Richards Bay and there was this split-wood fence running right around the field. Once you were inside, you had nowhere to run and we were a white team playing a black team in a black community in a country fraught with racial tensions. After the match, the local chief brought out the beers and we drank together like long-lost friends.

Football was well on its way and South African footballers broke down more barriers than any politician.

It was fantastic being a part of history.

Clive and Yvonne toast each other on their wedding day at the Plaza Hotel, Durban KZN, 28 October 1967. (Charles Bird)

TWO

A Different Life

*"Clive would dance with us, although not very well because he is
so bow-legged. But that was because he had big balls."*
– Lucas Radebe

Although football took up most of my attention and energy,
I can't admit to being focused solely on the sport in those
early days and there were forays into other avenues where
fame, success and money might follow.

I had bought a share in Reg Wright's Sports Shop in Montclair,
along with my good friend Charlie White and brother-in-law
Peter de Villiers, as well as a very astute businessman, Gerrit Perik.
Together, we owned a total of four sports shops – it was a good
period in my life.

At the time, my attention was pulled in the direction of horse-
racing. I owned a brown VW Beetle, which we would have used
to go to the races, but it had broken down, so four of us – Charlie,
Budgie Byrne, Henry Naudé and I – went in Charlie's car. He
complained that the brakes weren't all that great, but we insisted
we'd still get there, even if we had to make a plan not to hit
something at the bottom of a downhill. The only thing was that we
were going to Scottsville in Pietermaritzburg, an hour's drive from

Durban. Halfway back to Durban, we broke down when the car ran out of petrol and we had to push. It took much sweating and swearing before we managed to find a petrol station. Our legs ached for days afterwards.

I was also working at Kings Sports and Saturday was always our busiest day. Henry and I would alternate taking the jackpot each week, but because of the number of people on the floor, I didn't want to ask if I could go bet on the jackpot later that day. I still remember the name of the horse we backed; it would have been an upset and given us a huge win. Temujin had only won seven times from 73 starts and was a real outsider. But I never got the bet in.

There couldn't have been a more devastating outcome. Henry called me that evening in high spirits. Excitedly, he shouted down the phone, "We got it! We got it!"

But we didn't have it. I had to burst his bubble and tell him the truth. He never reminded me about it; I don't know if I would have been as gracious as him.

It was during this time that a group of us who played social Sunday League football were challenged to a rugby match against a side from Mount Edgecombe, a full-fledged rugby team, who came out wearing rugby jerseys, scrum caps and gum guards. We wore T-shirts.

At the first lineout, the ball went to one of our players and with eight huge rugby forwards bearing down on him, his language and skin took on a very colourful hue in anticipation of being the target of marauding forwards.

About 30 minutes into the game, after being scrummed into the ground and being offered a lineout or scrum by the referee, the whole team screamed at the top of their lungs: "LINEOUT!"

It was an education.

After receiving an almighty thumping, we challenged them to a game of cricket. Charlie had been taking all the catches and was put on the boundary for the last over. With all the well-lubricated supporters cheering and heckling him from behind, a huge shot was sent his way and, in the process of trying to catch the ball, he unfortunately palmed it over the rope for six. The bowler conceded 26 runs that over. We lost and Charlie never lived that down.

Our cricketing fervour never faltered, though. Charlie and I would play test series against each other at the Reg Wright Sports Shop and people would queue and just about pay good money to watch our antics in the shop. In one game Charlie hit the ball hard, it bounced off the ceiling, smashing Danny le Roux's glasses – he of Springbok, Durban City, Durban United and Arsenal fame.

We would hold wonderful discussions about politics and where South Africa was headed because, naturally, sport wasn't the only thing on our minds. There was always a fantastic buzz in the shop and if Durban City lost a match on the weekend, Grey Street wouldn't open until lunchtime; the Indian shopkeepers would all be at the Reg Wright Sports Shop, dissecting the outcome.

There was one guy, Kilroy, down on his luck, who we were forever chasing out the shop, because he would come in, grab something and bolt. Then one day he tried his trick, grabbed a pair of boots and sprinted out. Only, he didn't see the rope tied between two pillars to mark where painting was being done and the next thing he was on his back, out cold, having been clotheslined by the rope. We all thought he was dead.

Kilroy unintentionally gave us plenty of laughs during a really great time in our lives.

Boxing was also big at that time and we'd regularly watch bouts at Westridge Stadium, although we never paid to go in. The place had high fences and every six metres stood an AWB-type policeman with his dog. One evening Barry Barrett jumped the fence and missed a huge policeman by millimetres, landing instead on his Alsatian. About one second later, as if someone had pushed a Rewind button, he was back over the fence, having made an eight-foot leap an Olympic pole-vaulter would be proud of. Barry was the one who always argued that Mike Schutte was better than Muhammad Ali, that one punch from the South African would floor arguably the greatest boxer of all time. It was quite a statement to make, but he believed it.

Having been an enthusiastic spectator, it was only natural – or appeared that way – that I would get involved in boxing.

I was working at Reg Wright Sports Shop when Bernard Sikhepani, a boxer with a rather impressive six-pack, came in one day and demonstrated his fitness and skipping ability. When I asked whether he had a manager, he replied that he didn't and I suggested that I might be able to give him a hand.

On his debut down on Point Road, I rocked up in a cream three-piece suit with a blue shirt, looking very, very smart and rather dapper, as if my boxer were fighting in Las Vegas. My mates ragged me, suggesting that if I teased my hair into an afro I could pass as Don King.

After winning his first fight on points (against a very average boxer, it must be said), we promoted him as the greatest fighter of all time. But he lost his second, a tight bout against a boxer from Newcastle, and after two fights, we decided to call it a day.

Bernard became a builder and my Don King suit gathered dust at the back of my cupboard as I stuck to what I knew best: football. But there is no denying that from an early age, sport was in my blood.

Clive is true to himself, what you see is what you get. He has such a big heart – for anyone – for the players, the supporters; he had a soft touch for people. It's pure love for people and he has earned the kind of respect that makes people greet him affectionately when he walks down the street.

We both had knee problems and decided we would go and have operations together; I would check in at 6am in the morning and he would come in after me, at 6:30. I had booked in, was lying on the bed ready for surgery, but Clive was nowhere to be found. He hadn't arrived yet, but because he was always late I thought nothing of it. I went in for surgery and the first thought that came to mind when I came around was to ask after Clive. He hadn't come at all – he had sold me down the river and not for the first time.

– Butch Webster, player/manager (Durban City)

Clive on his farm in Richmond KZN,
with State Patrol, 1997.

THREE

Early Days

"Playing in that amateur setup was a stepping stone to playing for a Premier League team like Durban Bush Bucks or AmaZulu."
– JIMMY ORMSHAW

After my stint with Fynnlands, I moved to Pinetown Celtic in 1976, when Celtic's chairman, Snowy Vaubell, afforded me the opportunity to coach and guide the local team – one that had lofty aims.

We built the team through sheer hard work and common sense. The amateur setup was very strong and from it we were able to select quality, committed players so that both the local professional teams, Durban City and Durban United, stood to gain from the number of players who came through the amateur system.

Pinetown Celtic was a team with serious commitment and the results showed.

A lack of funds, though, made life very difficult for the club. For instance, we would fly in to Johannesburg on a Thursday, play a game that evening, recover on Friday and play again on Saturday afternoon. Perhaps we had the perfect ingredients in our recipe for success because we never lost an away game. It must have been the combination of playing hard, training lightly, patching up the players who had picked up injuries, scoring early and defending the right way. We certainly didn't have it easy, however. It was tough enough playing the sides from Joburg, but playing two games within 36 hours was a big ask. We'd have to request permission from local schools to use their fields so we could train.

All went well that season, right until the last game when we were up against Florida Albion, needing a win to ensure promotion. The game was played in Pinetown, just below the landmark Fields Hill, and rumour had it that Florida had negotiated with Troyville United to merge to ensure that a Joburg team would be promoted.

Florida played defensively and it looked like we would have to do all the attacking and running. When it appeared that we were running out of time to score the goal we needed to win the match late in the game, Terry Watson pressured the Albion defender to concede a corner kick. It was sent through the group of players gathered around the goal mouth and Terry side footed the ball into the bottom of the net – and with that, we won promotion into the big league. Terry was known as 'the dormouse' – he looked like one and was, pound for pound, the best player I had. He was in the Pinetown Celtic team that won the league and the Durban City team that won twice. His job description with Durban City was to mark Jomo Sono and he did a marvellous job, never failing me.

There were fantastic celebrations – until it came to our annual end-of-season dinner dance to honour the club and players as National League Second Division Champions. The presentation was to be held in Pinetown and, as with all amateur club end-of-year parties, the players, their wives and girlfriends and supporters rallied to celebrate.

That evening everyone was settled down for the presentation although no official business could start until our chairman had arrived, but there was no sign of Snowy. By around 8:30pm I eventually managed to get hold of him using a public telephone box – remember, there were no cellphones in those days – pointing out that we couldn't start the prize-giving without him.

He said he couldn't come. "What do you mean you can't come?" I asked. "You're the chairman of the club – you've got to be here."

At that point he broke down and started crying, explaining that we weren't going up as we didn't have the cash resources. We had won the league, but the mayor of Pinetown and City Council wouldn't provide financial support and had left us in the lurch.

The only way we could compete would be to play our games on Friday nights, because the weekends were shared by Durban City and Durban United. And if we were to play evening games, we'd need floodlights, which would be too expensive, certainly not affordable for our small club. Given that travel expenditure, wages and hotel expenses would take care of most of the available funds, putting up floodlights at the club would be impossible. The committee members would go to Greyville to bet on the horses and their winnings would go towards settling Pinetown Celtic's bar tab, but that was never going to be enough for lights and, anyway, they certainly never won enough.

I went to Snowy's house to fetch him and insisted that, no matter what, he had to face the guys, which, to his credit, he did. Among the tears and trauma, those at the prize-giving ceremony learned the club's fate: that we were out. It was sad that we never did move up and, unfortunately, missed an opportunity to create an avenue for young players to play in the big league.

While this was going on, due to the format of training – which in those days was just two sessions a week, unlike the modern-day professionalism where training is sometimes twice a day, and four to five times a week – you could be involved with the amateur team for two days and the other two days with the professional team and, in that way, handle two teams.

I had been coaching at AmaZulu as well as Pinetown Celtic, but at the end of the 1976 season, I shifted focus. Having played and coached at a higher level, I moved away from the professional ranks, back to the amateur setup, spending the next three years with Juventus.

I enjoyed coaching locally, because I felt the best footballers in the country came from KwaZulu-Natal and, to a degree, from other coastal areas such as Cape Town. The proof lies in the fact that the Under-14 and Under-16 KZN teams won the national tournaments regularly at that stage.

I was very happy coaching in KwaZulu-Natal. We had an amateur setup second to nobody in the world: classy, with well-prepared grounds and some outstanding footballers. The Premier League included clubs such as Stella, Ramblers, Juventus, Fynnlands, Pinetown, Virginia, Parkhill and Wanderers and was highly competitive. There were some fantastic players, many of whom went on to play pro football.

"Amateur football was very, very strong in those days and it was a natural progression for good players to then be selected to represent the province at Currie Cup level, after which the professional clubs got their hands on them," explains Jimmy Ormshaw, who played for Ramblers and was selected to play Currie Cup for Natal for two years in a row. "I then joined Clive at Bush Bucks in 1985 with about three months of the season remaining. They won the league before Clive went to AmaZulu and he took me across, where I played for six years."

Juventus was an Italian-supported club from Durban that competed in a top-class, well-organised and administered league, refereed by outstanding officials, notably Ian McLeod and father and son George and Jack Cox.

The club's chairman was a very dapper and talented businessman, Cleto di Paolo, and his right-hand man, Joe Pieri, the manager. Both their sons played for Juventus and Alex di Paolo still controls his father's business. Also worth mentioning are the three brothers Toni, Camillo and Nooch Torino, as well as Alex Byrne. Toni had a devastating left foot and got us out of many tight situations.

Valerio Chella was a top midfielder, left-footed without much speed, but he had the ability to slide past players. He could control the destiny of the game thanks to his good football brain and ability to dictate the pace of the match.

Another name that seems to have followed me is Neil Tovey, who captained Bafana Bafana, but back then, I didn't think much of his feet. They were huge and surely no self-respecting footballer could be light and nimble on such clumsy feet. When I saw this gangly young player walking towards me, my first thought was that he wouldn't be able to play football, that he wouldn't amount to much … How wrong I was. Neil had a huge heart, one that more than made up for his huge feet and, as his career soared, he would prove me wrong in the years ahead. I have never, to this day, been so wrong in my judgement.

I was very fortunate that I had an association with Clive from a young age, including way back in my younger days. Clive was working at Reg Wright Sports at the time and I'd pop in there and he probably thought, "How the hell can this bloke play football with such big feet!"

When Clive was coaching Juventus he invited me to play there when I first left school, in the months before I joined the army.

When I was in the army, there were only a couple of months that you played football. But in Durban you played through the whole season, so it was good for me to continue to play outside of army football and when he started coaching Durban City, I was based in Pretoria, but joined him there and would come down to play on weekends.

Following on from there, he joined Bush Bucks, then went to AmaZulu, and I moved from Durban City to AmaZulu. I then moved on to Chiefs before re-joining Clive with the national team and my association with him continued.

– Neil Tovey, former Bafana Bafana captain

Neil, who became the most successful Bafana Bafana captain of all time, possessed the outstanding ability to get the best out of his players and he could always turn a bad situation into a good one. I would watch him go and put his arm around each of the players in companionship and true brotherhood and would never ask them to do anything he wouldn't himself.

His only drawback was an innate inability to dance; he was no Fred Astaire or John Travolta.

My eldest son John also played for Juventus, having grown up playing for our local club, Yellowwood Park, which proved to be a good feeder to the next level of players, but probably the poorer cousin to the nearby teams of Ramblers and Wanderers.

At the age of 18, I was enjoying my soccer and playing probably the best I would ever play, aside from everything else I was doing as a teenager. My dad saw something in me and suggested that I could play if I were more focused. I took him up on that and went with him to Juventus, a really good team around that time, and to play for them was huge for me. It was very tough, being just 18 and the son of the coach and, because I really hate nepotism, I hated the idea that people would say I'd made it as a player because I was Clive Barker's son; I never wanted to play off my name.

It was great playing for Juventus and I believe I made the side purely on merit. However, there was always the pressure of being the coach's son and it was a tough year for the both of us. One of the difficulties was that I couldn't call him Dad on the training pitch, so I called him Clive, which I hated doing. But it would never have worked in the team environment if I referred to him, our coach, as "Dad". He was a tough coach, and hard on me and at a shooting practice for instance, I might shoot wide and my dad, who swore like a trooper, would let fly with a string of expletives. "My wife could kick harder than you, you #$%*," and my team-mates would rag me incessantly about my mother's superior footballing ability.

I didn't have a car at the time, so we'd drive back and forth together between Yellowwood Park and Botanical Gardens where Juventas trained and after a good training session or successful match, we'd stop off and buy peanuts and Cokes on the way home. When we'd won, the mood in the car would be great, but if we had lost or the training session went really badly, we would drive home in silence, the longest 20 minutes we could have endured in our lives. There were no peanuts, no Coke, no discussions. Just silence. However, looking back, it was a very special period in my life when my dad and I got to spend quality time together. I'm very grateful for that opportunity.

- John Barker, Clive's eldest son

It was really tough coaching my own son. It was terrible, because if he had played well I couldn't really go overboard in my praise of his performance, and if he played badly then I did go a bit overboard about it.

Eventually, there came a tough call to acknowledge that he deserved to play as first choice in his position, but I had to make that decision without it appearing that I was favouring my own son. I sat him down and explained that either he had to go or I had to go, one of the two. He went, returning to Ramblers; it was not a nice decision to have to make, but I think it was the sensible one.

Juventus were a special team – they could really play. It was a time when white football was starting to die at a professional level; there was no support and certainly no reason for it to continue and so it was on its way out. We took Juventus from the First Division into the Natal League and then into the Stella League.

Juventus, in their heyday, were one of the top club sides in Durban. Just as with their namesake in Italy, I knew it was important that when we put the structures together at the club, the team needed to be made up of a majority of Italian players and to that we added about 10 of the top amateur footballers in KwaZulu-Natal. We played with distinction; in our first year we ran second and the following year we won the league.

Once we had won our way through the amateur divisions and were making it into the big league, we were invited to the Natal League end-of-year presentation. On being called up to receive our trophy, Neil Finnigan, an ardent supporter of Stella (the Kaizer Chiefs of the amateur leagues), stood up and shouted, "Up this year, down the next!"

It didn't quite go down that way, but I guess Finnigan may have had the last laugh, even if he was wrong. Juventus finished runners-up the following year. To Stella.

We had a good thing going at Juventus. The mothers of the Italian players would make pasta and serve red wine. On the day we won the league, we sat in the changing room, surely the smallest ever built (but great because no one could talk behind your back without you hearing), and drank warm red wine to celebrate. I didn't drive home too well that night.

This was very much an Italian club, chaired and run by Italians, supported by Italians, but everyone understood and accepted that to be competitive there needed to be a mix of players, and were very accommodating when we suggested that this was the way the club needed to move.

With its Italian heritage, there was a bitter rivalry between Juventus and the Portuguese players of APN; in fact, it was more important to beat them than to lose to Stella.

One year an intercontinental competition was played, with sides representing English and Scottish players, and Juventus (Italy) and APN (Portugal) making up the other two sides.

An extremely volatile father of one of the Portuguese players from APN didn't like it when his son lost. He would be chased away because he came to the game with a pistol in the pocket of his shorts. Because the gun was so heavy, his pants would hang around his knees and he would stand on the far bank where he had a collection of rocks and stones ready to pelt at the referee should the official make a decision he didn't quite agree with. Of course players and spectators alike loved baiting him and one day someone shouted "Porta-Goose!" at him to rile him up and, boy, did he get upset. The next thing, he's firing shots in the air! He really had no sense of humour.

So although the white league seemed to be falling apart, the amateur leagues were getting stronger and stronger, and when I moved to Durban City, I was able to sign the best amateur players who had performed in the amateur leagues both for and against us in the previous two years. Many performed with distinction; Dave Kershaw was one. He was ill served by apartheid and could have played for any team in South Africa with great success, even representing the country.

It was during this period that Norman Elliott asked me to take over the coaching role at Durban City. I thanked him for the offer, but explained that I was too involved at Juventus. Not one to ever back off from getting what he wanted, Norman suggested a compromise: supervise just a couple of training sessions at Durban City.

I agreed.

Clive poses with the Durban City team and Miss South Africa in 1984. (Butch Webster)

FOUR

Durban City

*"We set a standard in the NPSL; some of the players had never had
that kind of discipline, but they soon got the message about the
professionalism we were instilling in the club."*
– BUTCH WEBSTER

B y the time that Norman Elliott, chairman of Durban City,
asked me to take on the coaching role in 1980, I already had
some experience of the club. I had played for the Blue and
Whites between 1959 and 1961 and City had since moved from the
popular Federation League to join the sleeping giant, the National
Professional Soccer League, which was to ultimately become
today's Premier Soccer League.

This was the time when the sport was beginning to breach the
race barrier between white and black, signalling the start of many
changes that would be made to the League structure.

At the end of the 1977 season the white National Football
League was disbanded and the teams from the 'white' league were
invited to join the National Professional Soccer League, which
boasted those giants of Soweto: Kaizer Chiefs, Orlando Pirates
and Moroka Swallows. Durban City refused on the basis of our
sizable and fanatical support among the Indian population, which

had helped drive our success and who may not support us against the Soweto sides – as did Hellenic, Dynamos and Cape Town City – and, instead, joined the Federation League, including the likes of Manning Rangers and Santos. Durban City went on to win the Federation League in 1978 and it appeared that they would be lost to the new, unified league, but the NPSL administrators knew that for football to be unified, all the top former white clubs had to be included and, in the end, sanity prevailed; in the 1979 season, Durban City, Hellenic, Dynamos and Cape Town City were included in a 16-team league, which was won by Kaizer Chiefs.

The following year Highlands Park won the League and the unification process was finally complete – a former NFL team had won the 'unified league'. In that 1979 season, City finished a respectable sixth on the table, but found the going tough, finishing tenth in 1980.

As the league became more and more professional, Durban City, run on limited resources, was always going to struggle against the well-financed likes of Chiefs, Pirates, Wits and Highlands. They struggled for most of the season and looked to be fighting a relegation battle, when the phone call came from Norman, inviting me to join Durban City.

I saw it as a golden opportunity to finally coach a mixed-raced team that was competing at the highest level of the game in South Africa. I was intrigued to merge the two styles of football into one unit.

Norman Elliott and I had worked together with the petroleum giant Mobil Oil to devise a coaching programme for them, so I wasn't stepping into completely new territory. This was still very much a time of segregation; although there was a lot of positive stuff happening, particularly in the football world, times were still very tough for black players, who would be ferried to the old Kingsmead football stadium by bus before we put them through an introductory training session. The players then returned home to the townships.

When I arrived at Durban City's training ground for the first time, I discovered to my consternation that fewer than 12 players had pitched up. I asked Norman Elliott if this was the best he had – in the entire group of players, there were no more than four or five decent talents – and, if that was so, he was in trouble because Durban City were down to play Wits University away that Saturday. As the game drew nearer, more and more City players began to withdraw and I feared that we wouldn't even be able to field a full team.

So it was that I phoned Butch Webster and begged him to play. He was at Florida Albion at the time and City had pipped them twice so I couldn't be sure Butch could even be coaxed to join the enemy. Butch was one of the players I enjoyed riling up because he was a hothead on the field and I doubt he felt too much love for me.

I'd never had an opposition coach swear me out as much as Clive did, so when I received his phone call, his voice was the last I expected to hear.

Clive always made sure his team got me going. One of the first instances I remember was a match being played at Florida Albion when he sent on a player to target me, get me going and get me sent off. When the guy came on, he spat at me, but the first time he received the ball, I launched an attack on him, tackled him hard and put him back on the bench.

But in my heart, I'd always loved Durban although I lived in Johannesburg, and the next thing Clive called me and said he wanted me to come down to the coast. My circumstances then meant that the timing wasn't really right, although I was honoured that Clive had thought of me in that way.

I had to make a decision, but because I lived in Johannesburg, I ended up signing for Wits University with Eddie Lewis. The season continued for about six months before Clive called me again and said to me, "I need someone to come down here - would you be interested?" I spoke to Eddie Lewis and he was really nice about it, telling me he would never stand in my way. I wanted to take a chance, so I accepted his offer. I flew to Durban and met Clive and Graham Wilson at the Blue Waters Hotel where we discussed the deal. Wits were okay with me leaving and I came to play for Clive.

– Butch Webster

I now had Butch, and was quick to secure Stephen Jarrett, who had just finished his military duty, and he and Alan Wasserman joined the team for the big match that weekend. I stayed behind in Durban with Juventus, but scores were relayed back to me, and at half-time the score was 0–0. As Alan Watt, the City goalkeeper, ran past the Wits technical team for the start of the second half, he heard one of the staff mutter, "This must be one of the worst Durban City teams I've ever seen," to which Alan retorted, "I think we're doing pretty well seeing as we only have 10 players in our squad and some of them didn't even pitch up for the game."

Right at the end of the match, Wits scored to win 1–0, but what an effort from the Durban City boys. Butch had played with a heavily strapped knee and earned a bust lip, Stephen cramped up badly and Alan was playing in his first match for the team.

Things were about to change.

With the introduction of Marco Minetti, City could boast a talented striker in their line-up. Marco was able to turn on a tickey. He was quick as lightning, brave, great in the air and had the ability to hit the ball with both feet. He was City's go-to man. And to top it all off, he was very good looking and of the modern era, not unlike the incomparable Ronaldo.

At a prize-giving one year, Marco was presented with a Datsun Pulsar for his goal-scoring exploits and the whole of the Durban City team escorted him to the function to honour the winners. Dennis Wicks, our spokesman, then suggested we all meet at Slippers Boogie Palace to celebrate, but one of the players reminded us that no blacks, Indians or coloureds would be allowed inside. So, together, the team decided to break the law and we made our way to the Los Angeles Hotel in Musgrave.

Dennis put a pretty convincing case forward and the nightclub manager eventually allowed us in. It was astonishing that the authorities would allow black and white to unite on a football field, but as soon as the match or training was over, apartheid laws would be enforced and we would have to go our separate ways.

Marco was always going to attract attention and he was duly scouted and offered trials with two overseas clubs. With his sublime ability to turn off both feet and being too quick for his own good, I always thought he would pick up injuries – and he eventually suffered a knee injury before returning to South Africa to play for Juventus under Mike Makaab. Sadly, he was a shadow of his former self.

Although Butch had hung up his boots as a player, I knew the type of person he was and I wanted him back with the club. At the time, the Federation League was still running, but in opposition to the NPSL, and Butch had grown tired of the politics, retiring from football to tackle the Comrades Marathon.

"I'd always loved Durban City; from the time I was a kid, I remember listening to Reg Wright reporting on Sundays," Butch explains, "and a return was not necessarily out of the question."

I approached Butch with an offer … Would he consider making a comeback? I knew Norman would be completely opposed to that idea, insisting that Butch would never kick a ball for his team while he was there, but I felt that he did not have much of an option at that point: the club wasn't doing well; in fact, it was in terrible shape and Norman owed the players six months' wages. Times were tough and it appeared that we were going to be relegated.

When I met Norman Elliott at his Durban North home to discuss the way forward with Durban City, I mentioned that I wanted the most organised manager that I had ever worked with, Butch Webster. Norman nearly fell off his chair in shock. "I would never work with Butch; he'd be a threat going into the townships," he told me. He felt that Butch couldn't control his temper – and he was right. Butch hated losing and we would often point out the blue vein that popped out on his neck when his temper flared.

I told Norman that if he wanted my help to keep the club in the first division, I would only do it if he made Butch the manager. I didn't want to have to deal with the press or player issues – I just wanted to coach the team.

Butch was a team man who loved his players and I pushed hard for him. Also at the meeting was Norman's friend, Chokie Angel, who agreed with me and, outnumbered, Norman finally relented and withdrew his reservations, accepting Butch's appointment.

That was the start of a fantastic partnership. There were only 10 games left that year and we worked hard to regroup for the remainder of the season. We were short of players and it was a nightmare, but we hung on by one point and managed to avoid relegation. The following year Butch and I put our heads together and I think the combination really worked. We knew each other's strengths and weaknesses and came up with a plan. Butch insisted that we enforce discipline, and promptly drew up rules and regulations that every player had to adhere to.

The last games of that first season saw us settling down, just trying to stay in the first division. Fortunately, the players seemed okay with the idea of Butch taking on the role of player/manager, but the two of us agreed that we needed to get some quality players because we were a bit thin on talent, particularly if we wanted to fulfil our goals for the club.

I think much of our success was thanks to Butch being such an organised manager, certainly the best I had ever worked with, due largely to his ability to get the best out of his players. Also to his credit was his attitude towards his supporters and the all-important sponsors and how well he performed his duties as the liaison between the chairman and coach, not to mention his relationship with the press.

Together, Butch and I scouted the best amateur players, targeting the best local players, and Butch would go and talk to them and get the contracts signed.

Norman Elliott was smart; because he knew he had to consider how the other players would react to Butch filling the role as manager as well as player, he sent Butch to England. Butch had played with Gary Bailey at Wits and it was through Gary that he managed to arrange an English coaching course for a week – not to coach, but to allow Butch to upskill himself. He spent a week with Jack Taylor, the World Cup referee at Wolverhampton, who helped him better understand advertising and sponsors, and then a week with Graham Taylor at Watford, who welcomed him with open arms, treating him like one of the group, letting him sit in at the team talks. In Graham's office was a quote on the wall: *Happy are those who dream and pay the price to make their dreams come true.*

That stuck with Butch because his dream had always been to play for Durban City. He finally spent a week at Manchester United before returning to South Africa with all this knowledge.

Armed with the experience gained in England, we enforced a real sense of professionalism. We applied strict rules; 11pm was bedtime and there were to be no exceptions. When we played away from home, we would share rooms to save money and Butch and I were always roommates – there was no special treatment for anyone, including management. The bellmen knew us, knew the team, and I would whisper to them to let us know if they saw any of the players doing something wrong. We had played football ourselves and knew all the tricks. Often we would get a late call to come down to the hotel bar, where the players would be caught out, but vehemently deny they were drinking anything stronger than tea. They'd be fined – those proved to be the most expensive cups of tea they ever drank. The players resented it and I would then have to try to motivate a disgruntled team. Sometimes I would be the one to catch them, then it would fall on Butch to give them a boost; we played the good-cop-bad-cop scenario pretty well.

It wasn't only about juggling manager duties with playing, but eventually, something had to give. We were training one Wednesday when I felt after the session that I had lost the edge. Clive was trying to control the players and I wasn't doing what I thought I should be doing, so I said to Clive that I was done, and that I'd manage full time and he'd coach.

From there, we set a standard in the NPSL; we dressed the same, we even had going-away outfits. I would never allow a player to be photographed without his Adidas kit on – they were our sponsors at the time and phenomenal about it. Some of the players had never had that kind of discipline; they'd be fined for being five minutes late and Clive backed me all the way. They soon got the message about the professionalism we were instilling in the club.

I'd never known any other coach like Clive who had the ability to motivate players and really grind them to get the best out of them. He's a people's person and his players all loved playing for him.

– Butch Webster

Butch was a true professional and would provide us with an in-depth, minute-by-minute schedule of movements from the time we arrived at the airport to the time we got back. The setup at Durban City was far ahead of anyone else, although it wasn't always serious. On plane trips, the players would take over the public-address microphone and make announcements or sing, and have everyone on the plane singing the whole way back home.

In that first year of our partnership, in 1980, we saved the team from relegation; the following year we came tenth in the league; then in '82 we won the league – and again the following year.

That was a very special era, an incredible partnership that had started with me baiting Butch as a player, swearing at him in every game I was involved against him, and then getting him to come play for me. I knew that he would run through a brick wall for me. We became great friends, and over 35 years later we remain so.

Butch was the first successful manager I worked with and together we built a magnificent team that was going places.

The culmination of this success was reaching the Cup Final and playing Kaizer Chiefs in 1984. Durban City had gone on to the semifinal of the BP Top 8, and the League's PRO Abdul Bhamjee realised that this was a chance to make real money. Chiefs were playing Wits in the second game, so he asked us to go up to Joburg to play Moroka Swallows – with just one aim: he wanted a Chiefs–Swallows final. He figured that Swallows would end our run and he'd get his dream final.

With our striker Kevin Mudie scoring a hat trick, we went on to win comfortably 4–1, which upset Bhamjee's plan. We had really thrown the cat among the pigeons by putting on a wonderful performance to qualify for the final.

After the match, Norman put his arm around me and suggested we go watch the second game. He confided in me that there were two things he was praying for: firstly, that Chiefs beat Wits in the semifinal so we would meet them in the final, and secondly, he hoped and prayed that Chiefs beat us. That way, Durban City would earn a match fee, but he wouldn't have to pay any bonuses out of it. That was typical of Norman, but he was fabulous for the game and I'm so sorry he will never get to read this book.

The final was played in Soweto, but unlike Abdul, Norman was granted his wish and Durban City lost.

Aside from possibly Abdul Bhamjee, Norman had no peer in soccer. Norman took football to the highest level in Durban. The stadium would be full and, in the case of a local derby between Durban City and Durban United, there would be a build-up all week. Norman, making money for the club, pushed and manipulated the hype – very successfully too.

Norman Elliott loved publicity and worked out he could make lots of money from football so he let me do my own thing to promote the games. I remember offering a goat to Jomo Sono – someone else I cannot speak more highly of – if he played against Durban City. I wanted to draw a big crowd and Jomo was a crowd-puller, frequently filling stadiums. Any team who played against Chiefs, Pirates and, to a lesser extent, Moroka Swallows, all cashed in.

After Jomo led his side to victory against Durban City he walked across to me and, in front of the crowd, asked where his goat was. Although Jomo never did get the goat, I did not renege on my promise because Ron Philips, the PRO for Tongaat Huletts, would call me each Monday to ask me to remove Jomo's goat, which was raiding the gardens. I kept putting him off and the goat continued to roam the estate. Jomo and I met recently at a funeral and afterwards he referred to the goat I offered him over 35 years ago and jokingly asked when we were going to fetch it.

When Norman decided to take the club into the Federation, Durban City played fantastic football that season to win the league, so Norman made the decision to remain with the Federation. Most of the supporters in the Federation were Indian and Norman attracted big crowds of Indian supporters to watch his beloved Durban City play. It was clear that the normalisation of football in South Africa was starting to take place, but the world would not buy into it until Nelson Mandela was released and there was a corresponding change within the country itself.

Footballers were nevertheless making a statement. One year we had an issue when Durban City received a letter from the city council stating that the Military Tattoo would be taking over our facility. Natal Rugby didn't want horses running on the Kings Park field, but we were top of the log at the time so Norman confronted the city council, who suggested we simply move our home-ground matches to the township for six weeks. I wonder what Sir Alex Ferguson would make of a demand to temporarily move his team from Old Trafford to some other venue …

Norman was a top-class businessman, readily able to make it to the front page of just about every newspaper. That finally happened when he moved Durban City into the big league, featuring Kaizer Chiefs and Orlando Pirates, but still it was mainly white teams playing the likes of Chiefs, Pirates and Moroka Swallows, the big clubs at the time.

If Durban City played Durban United, there would be the best part of 40 000 supporters in the stands. But, although the white teams had elected to remain in their leagues, everything eventually started to fall into place and there were some wonderful matches. These big games attracted a lot of attention, but as long as people weren't using football to further their political aims, the National Party government – usually so Big-Brotherish – tended to leave the sport to its own devices. With that said, however, my association with football in the townships and my close association with African sporting personalities did me no favours as a white man. The National Party, forever looking for spies under beds and communists behind every corner, sent their own spies to keep an eye on me. A white man spending so much time in black townships was bound to mean trouble in a political system that had produced apartheid and I firmly believe that the cars parked near our home for hours on end were government agents.

Norman was South Africa's Mr Football. He would often appear on the front page of the newspapers – for both good and bad reasons. He could stir things up, but he also knew when to back off. He never interfered with team selection, although there was one occasion when he wanted to get a black player to play for us, and that indeed caused a problem.

Excellent Mthembu was the player we were after, but I knew he wasn't quite ready. Norman, however, sensed the opportunity for publicity and I remember him coming into our changing room – the only time he ever did. The headline in the *Sunday Tribune* that day claimed that Excellent was going to make his debut for Durban City. I turned to Butch and said no ways – he wasn't ready to play and it would be too great a responsibility on his young shoulders in such a big game, a showcase for him as well as the team. I pointed out that we had to be careful about what we were doing, that we were forcing the issue. So Norman told our captain Mark Tovey to have a chat with me; he needed the kid to play, he said. I immediately ordered Norman out of the dressing room. Naturally, he refused, so I said: "Either you go, or I do." As he walked out – not before a verbal tirade and a few choice expletives on my part – he fumed that I had no respect for anyone. Excellent didn't play that day, although he would later represent the club.

Norman may have pushed the boundaries when he sensed that he or the club could gain from it, but he also accepted that discretion was sometimes the better part of valour. And he would know. Under his stewardship, the club had been forced to negotiate stormy waters, some really tough times.

The club had been in financial trouble when we had taken over as coach and manager – in fact, Durban City was virtually bankrupt; they owed everyone. But somehow we managed to pick the right players, people and personalities and put them together, and we were thus able to save the club. We paid back every single debt, even resorting to selling one of our good players to do so, but we honoured everything.

During the time Butch and I ran Durban City, Norman didn't always like it, but we made sure every player was paid and were thus able to turn Durban City back into the glamour club it had always been.

With that said, though, if we hadn't attracted the crowds we did, we would have battled to stay afloat. We'd play Kaizer Chiefs in Soweto in front of a huge crowd of 60 000 people and be paid our share of the gate takings in cash. There would be huge energy around the games, and although the cash payment we received would generally turn out to be about half of what we expected, it was still better than nothing.

Norman had a reputation for being something of a Silver Fox, of stiffing players. I think his belief in life was that if you weren't producing something for him, you weren't of much use to him. Butch and I fought for an injured player, Mike Lundsman, when he couldn't play for nine months and every month Butch – the only manager given the responsibility of signing cheques for Norman – wrote a cheque to Mike and he and Norman would fight about it.

Because the club was struggling financially, we agreed to play double-headers in Johannesburg and Cape Town. We would travel to those cities and play on a Friday night, stay over and then play again on the Sunday, all for our portion of the gate takings – testimony as to how fit this bunch of amateurs really were.

Then, as the club started to progress, sponsors started taking notice. Sanyo was one and, with their support, we had the opportunity to bring out Mick Channon of Southampton fame, who also went on to represent the English national football team. Mick was one of the top English strikers at the time and he played for us for a six-game period. He was also a horse-racing fanatic and, after retiring from a very successful footballing career, went on to become a racehorse trainer.

One typically warm and humid Friday afternoon in Durban, I asked who would be fetching Mick to bring him to training as he didn't have a car, but no one could find him. So I said I would start the training without him. About 15 or 20 minutes later, here comes Mick, in his tracksuit, jogging a little unsteadily from one or two liquid refreshments.

We were doing a shooting exercise at the time, where I would receive the ball, then play it on for Mick to shoot at. That afternoon, he hit more pigeons in the sky than the back of the net. Butch's golden boy in action!

Mick was a real character, although he did leave us with a massive R6000 bill for racing bets.

I think it was the honesty and hard work that made my partnership with Butch Webster such a success. We were completely loyal to each other and, just as I wouldn't interfere with his work, he wouldn't interfere with mine. I think that was the reason we were so successful: we would do most things off the cuff but never stepped into the other's field. We built a bit of an empire really, but we worked very hard and we won the league the honest way. We were very fortunate to have someone like Norman Elliott, though. For all he had to say about Butch, Norman really loved him. He trusted Butch implicitly. Butch looked after the fortunes of Durban City and did so admirably and very successfully.

It was a great time to be a part of Durban City Football club. Durban City were a team that would fight for anything, always in with a chance. They should have won the league in 1984 when I was already at Bush Bucks. I say *should* have won, but for a penalty given against them in the last 30 seconds of the final game of the season.

It wasn't the first time Chiefs earned a questionable penalty, nor the last. Marks Maponyane has given me his word that he will back up an incident back in 1982 when Durban City met Chiefs in a league match that would determine the overall league champions.

As Marks was running into the box, the referee ran behind him saying, "Dive in the box, dive in the box," which he did – and the penalty was duly awarded. Wagga Wagga Likoebe, a prolific goal-scorer for Chiefs, stepped up to take the penalty and then struck it over the crossbar.

I thought that was justice well served.

Clive being introduced by D Kruger of John Player Special ahead of JPS final between Durban Bush Bucks and Kaizer Chiefs. (Deon Pieterse)

FIVE

Bush Bucks

"I look back at that time under Clive at Bush Bucks with a lot of happiness, a lot of joy and immense pride. I played with some great people, under a fantastic coach like Clive."
– CALVIN PETERSEN

After winning the league twice with Durban City, at the end of the 1983 season I moved on.

I had the Puma agency, given to me by Roy Eckstein, and he called me in and asked if I'd consider taking over Bush Bucks. I met up with Butch and discussed my prospects with him and told him I wanted to move on. He argued that I couldn't leave, that we had this special relationship and friendship and I'd be crazy to give it all up. I explained that I would receive double the salary I was earning at Durban City. But I was not leaving City just for the money – the move to Bush Bucks would also cement my relationship with Puma and Roy Eckstein.

The financial offer from Bush Bucks put an end to the partnership with Butch and the hardest thing for me was telling him I was going to accept it. I think he saw merit in my decision and wished me well.

When I am asked which team was the best I ever coached – and this has happened often – I'm sure they expect me to say the Bafana Bafana team that won the 1996 Africa Cup of Nations. Truth be told, there are three teams in the running for the best South African club side ever: one is the 1992/93/94 Kaizer Chiefs side and the second is the Orlando Pirates team that conquered Africa in 1995. But in reality – and without a shadow of doubt – the Bush Bucks team I coached in 1985 was by far the best side ever seen in this country.

Kaizer Motaung will argue with that, and Irvin Khoza might suggest that that acclaim belongs to the famous 1995 Orlando Pirates side. But Bush Bucks could have played backwards and beaten both teams.

We played Orlando Pirates in the very first match at the official opening of the Ciskei football stadium and I remember looking up at the scoreboard after 20 minutes. It read Bush Bucks 5, Orlando Pirates 0. We went on to win 7–2 in a match played in a fantastic atmosphere.

Big scores were regular occurrences then, due largely to the quality of footballer we had as well as the successful football we played.

Lawrence Ngubane, the Big Bear, charming and charismatic, knew every player in the country and knew who could win you a championship. He set up a Bush Bucks team that was to be the envy and talk of the whole country. He was instrumental, too, in assembling the very cosmopolitan side with international players from all over the world. But good football man that he was, he would always willingly listen to my suggestions.

During the off-season, I was overseas on a skiing holiday in Neustift im Stubaital in the Austrian state of Tyrol with my wife Yvonne and some friends when the phone rang at 6am one morning. I panicked, convinced that the only time someone would phone me overseas (at that hour) would be to tell me that something had happened to my kids. But it was Lawrence, asking me which striker I wanted. Once I had composed myself and turned my mind to his question, I suggested that he hadn't given me much time to even think about it.

"Just give me the name of your player," he urged, so I said, "I think the best striker is Mike Mangena; but do me a favour, I'm on holiday so please wait until I get back. But if you're going to buy a player, buy Mike Mangema." Which he did. Mike scored 25 goals the next season – 15 with the head – and was arguably the best striker in the country at that stage.

Of course Lawrence didn't leave it there. The following day the phone rang again: "Which central defender do you want?" I said, "Lawrence, I thought I was on holiday but I might as well still be in South Africa! Okay, Ian Chester would be the guy I'd go for. But you pick." And of course Ian Chester joined us.

This team had perfect balance: Dave Watterson in goals, Mark Tovey, Ian Chester, Raul Gonzalez – who played internationally for Chile – and Stuart Turnball from Scotland at the back; a wonderful threesome in the midfield, with the dynamic Mlungisi 'Professor' Ngubane, the best controller of a football I have ever seen, full of skill and style; Dennis Wicks, who had a work rate without peer; and Daniel Ramarutsi. Upfront we had a very special strike-force comprising Calvin Petersen, Mike Mangena and Bennett Gondwe on the left wing. I don't think we used more than 14 players that entire season.

We were professional in every way and probably the only team in KwaZulu-Natal that paid wages on time. We were the envy of every team and could play better than anyone. Our record speaks for itself.

"That was a fantastic side. I was just a youngster on the fringes who played a handful of games towards the end of the season, but the sheer professionalism opened my eyes, even if we only trained three days a week while we held down a job, then played on the weekend," explains Jimmy Ormshaw.

"It was a very happy bunch of guys. When you have such talented team-mates and you're playing such great football, and you're winning the league, the team can't be anything but happy. It was like playing in an All-Stars club."

I know there was no other side that could play like them. They won the league without losing a match – or lost the last game when it didn't matter. We would fill the stadiums and we dominated the football scene at the time.

> The reason why that team was so successful was because of the players Clive and Lawrence Ngubane were able to attract. When I started there in 1984, Clive showed Lawrence a list of players he wanted to get in and said with that team we could win the league.
>
> It was so amazing that even with all the players coming in from different places, different teams and even overseas countries, he managed to make everyone fit in. From the word go, we played Kaizer Chiefs and hammered them 5-0, we put four or five goals past Pirates. That team was unstoppable because of what he made the players believe.
>
> We would walk on the field and the opposition would look at us in fear.
>
> More than 50% of the players that he asked Lawrence to get in were from outside, but what was so amazing was how the team just gelled together.
>
> We went unbeaten for about 35 games, including friendly matches. I think we lost to Aces and possibly one other game in that season. It was an outstanding team, the players were a different breed and it wasn't difficult to coach us because we were so intelligent. That was important because the players could understand him and relate to what he was telling us.
>
> Training itself was like a championship match because the competition was so fierce. The players weren't dirty, but we went in hard; nobody wanted to lose at training. Professor Ngubane, for example, was never much of a runner, but the way that man ran showed what the training was all about. And we got support from each other, there was no jealousy; it didn't matter if you were black, pink, white or blue, it was all about camaraderie.
>
> I still recall photos of Prof lying in between Ian Chester and Mark Tovey. There was no colour issue, even though this was right in the dark days of the apartheid era. Clive was

instrumental in this culture of equality.

He was not about colour, he just wanted you to play in his team, it was about the person you were and that's very important because many coaches don't have that kind of man management skill, which seemed to come so easily for Clive. He could joke with the players, he wanted to be with the players. But we had a lot of respect for him.

He knew how to treat individual players, those that gave him a difficult time got it right back.

– Calvin Petersen, player (Bush Bucks and Bafana Bafana)

The chairman of Bush Bucks, Mandlonke Mbili, was also the owner of a butchery. He couldn't read or write, but he made a lot of money selling his meat at the Dalton Hostel in lower Umbilo. Every Monday, following a win on the Saturday or Sunday, we would gather around him, breathing in the smell of mince meat left out for a few days to ripen.

Then he would perform his favourite trick. As we all lined up, he would give a cabaret performance on how to cut meat and would throw the meat in extravagant fashion onto a sheet of brown paper and you'd have to hand over your R2.

This wasn't a win bonus – you had to pay for it. Of course, there was no querying the quantity of meat for R2; if you stood there and hesitated, he would throw the meat back onto the counter; you'd miss out and he'd shout to the next person in line. Nothing was going to stop the cabaret show.

When Bucks played Kaizer Chiefs in the JPS Cup Final, we were drawn to play the first leg of the double-header in Durban, with a capacity crowd witnessing first-class football and a narrow win by Chiefs.

The second leg of the final, to be played at Ellis Park in

Johannesburg, very nearly didn't take place because earlier that day the players decided to boycott the final. Professor Ngubane, Mark Tovey and Dave Watterson asked to address the directors to ask for more money.

Bush Bucks had a wealthy and powerful band of directors: Harry Spain and Dr Julian Frankel, chaired by business tycoon Roy Eckstein of Puma fame; and after I explained the situation to Harry, he suggested I book the players out of their hotel and drive back to Durban. He said Chiefs could win the trophy by default.

The players turned a less-than-delightful shade of green and red and had a quick rethink. They went onto the field and played to a draw, losing the final on the all-important away goal rule.

No-nonsense Harry Spain had called their bluff and won the day.

Calvin Petersen looks back on his playing days at Bush Bucks with great fondness, and one incident in particular.

I was owed money by the club and they didn't want to pay me. On the day of the game - we were playing Swallows - I went to Clive and said to him: "CB, I'm not playing today." He asked me what was wrong and I told him I hadn't been paid the money owing to me. I explained that I had come to the game because I was serious about playing for the club but it wasn't right that they hadn't paid me. He asked how I could do it and I said that I wasn't being full of nonsense, but I also had to survive. "What can I do?" he asked. I responded that he should speak to the club officials and get them to pay me what was due to me, because if I didn't make a stand, it was going to happen again.

So he suggested that he write something down on paper, a guarantee to pay me, and I said if that was the case then yes, I'd play. So he took a serviette and wrote on it, "If you don't get your money, I will pay you out of my own pocket." I played, we won 4-0 and I scored twice. On Monday, the money came.

He was an amazing coach. A very passionate man.

– Calvin Petersen

Unfortunately it all ended because we were unable to keep the team together; if you assemble a side like that, it is going to cost you a lot of money and everyone was milking it as best they could.

Billy McGillivray and David Dlamini had asked to pick my brain over which team of players I would select were I in charge of AmaZulu. The team I named included Calvin Petersen and Mark Tovey, among others. Mark was already heading to Kaizer Chiefs and we'd sold Mike Mangema back to Sundowns, so the great Bush Bucks team was already starting to break up. Roy Eckstein, in his wisdom, wanted to know why I couldn't merge AmaZulu with Bush Bucks to dominate South African football.

The directors envisaged a fantastic opportunity to make lots of money because Bush Bucks had the team, AmaZulu had support in vast numbers, and the directors believed I could mix that. They were confident that I had the ability to get both teams to play together, but I argued that it was impossible.

What Roy didn't take into account, and I explained it to him, was the fact that Bush Bucks attracted largely Xhosa and Ponda supporters and it was impossible to merge them with the Zulu-based team.

When AmaZulu and Bush Bucks played each other, I would go into the changing rooms and there would be assegais and knobkerries wrapped in blankets; there was no way they could ever work together.

Following the second meeting, in which we discussed the desired player issue, the *Ilanga* newspaper jumped out and took a picture of me with the AmaZulu opposition. That weekend was the start of the friendly matches ahead of the season and as I arrived at the game, the Bush Buck supporters began hissing at me, "Wena inyoka!" [You're a snake!] and giving me a hard time. Butch Webster, playing for Chiefs then, suggested I go home because I wasn't very popular at that moment.

On the night of the presentation after we had won the league, I resigned to go back to AmaZulu – who subsequently ran third in the league the following season, behind Bush Bucks in second and Rangers who won.

We had had a fantastic run at Bush Bucks, playing in numerous cup finals, but unfortunately that was the end of arguably the best team ever seen in South Africa. Certainly one of the best I've ever coached. To this day, I still ask myself how we managed to let things go like that. What a pity Bush Bucks weren't around a little longer, at the time when football was changing. At a meeting in Glenwood, it was finally decided that the team would be sold, but I have no doubt that this team would have broken all kinds of records had we managed to retain the same talent. Sadly, the team no longer exists, which is a real tragedy.

I did, however, return to Bush Bucks 10 years later when the new owners enticed me there, but spent only a short period with the team. Roy Eckstein and Harry Spain had left after I made it clear that an amalgamation of AmaZulu and Bush Bucks was impossible and I knew there were going to be problems because, although Lawrence could patch it up and keep it going, he couldn't run the football team on his own. He still did a wonderful job under trying circumstances.

So the directors who had propped up the once-famous Black-and-Gold team had left and the club was in deep financial trouble. Players from Pietermaritzburg hadn't been paid and were threatening to refuse to travel to play in Joburg.

One evening during training, a big, flashy and very expensive-looking sports car pulled up and Lawrence introduced me to a couple who invited me to visit their nightclub after training. Lawrence suggested I phone Yvonne and tell her I wasn't going to be home early. I asked if he was sure and he responded that it would be a good idea because they had lots of money.

When we arrived at the nightclub in Stanger Street, I ordered a drink and Lawrence his customary tea while we sat watching everybody gliding smoothly over the dance floor. I was getting impatient at the lack of any formal discussion with the owners, but Lawrence said to play along because he wanted them to join the club as directors. The club needed the cash to help get through tricky financial times.

Eventually, at about 11pm, we were summoned to their offices and pleasantries exchanged before one of the two owners, Lynn Johnson, launched into a lecture about how Lawrence and I should be running and coaching a professional football team because she didn't think we were doing a very good job. By this point, I'd had enough and it clearly showed because Lawrence kicked me under the table and gave me a stern look that suggested I hold my tongue and let him do the talking. Perhaps the word 'suggested' doesn't quite explain the emotion he was clearly trying to convey.

So I kept silent, but inside I was seething as Lynn invited two university students to explain to us how they would improve the image, functioning and general success of the club – which would have been all very well if we had directors pumping money in.

The students must have known something, though, because Lynn then went over to her safe, unlocked it, pulled out a huge wad of cash and handed it to a very jubilant Lawrence. Lawrence glanced over at me with a wink that was either pure, unadulterated relief or – as I prefer to think – suggested that he knew better than me.

The Johnsons were a delightful couple who had lots and lots of money, but they didn't last too long in the game.

The Big Bear had, however, crossed another bridge to keep Bush Bucks alive.

When he eventually crossed yet another bridge, this time to Joburg, I mentioned to Irvin Khoza that Lawrence was Orlando Pirates' best signing. Lawrence went on to great things with Pirates, particularly with regard to the influence the club had in the make-up of the 1996 Africa Cup of Nations Bafana Bafana side. He went on, too, to win many league and cup victories with the famous Black-and-White team. He and Irvin – both great personalities who served our local and international football team with distinction – remained friends until Lawrence sadly passed away in late 2016.

Clive soaks up the sun ahead of South Africa's match against England at Old Trafford in Manchester. (Matthew Ashton/PA Images)

SIX

AmaZulu

*"The 1992 and 1993 seasons were probably the best
AmaZulu ever had."*
– George Dearnaley

L ife is full of strange twists and turns and with the low points come the highlights. Success is never far away, although sometimes that gap between winning and losing is immeasurably wide and unattainable. AmaZulu were probably the most successful team to never win a trophy between 1972 and 1992. But that's a cup final for you.

My relationship with AmaZulu was a bit of a merry-go-round, coaching them a number of times between 1974 and 1976, and then more recently in 1985–87, 1992–93 and finally between 1997 and 1999.

AmaZulu was a wonderful club, a team just waiting for something special to happen. I knew AmaZulu could win – they were certainly good enough – and we eventually delivered when we won the Coca-Cola Cup, beating Kaizer Chiefs in the final in 1992, just before I joined Bafana Bafana.

Politically, and on the sports field in particular, things were heating up during the late 1970s. Football in particular started to make a statement and people were beginning to challenge the government, asking why the black majority couldn't represent rugby and cricket; but it was the football fraternity that really started implementing the changes.

This was the beginning of the move from an all-white setup to encouraging black fans to come and watch the games. Durban City's Norman Elliott was influential here because he had two interests: firstly, he wanted to offer the best football and, secondly, he knew how much money he was going to make.

This was also the start of the era of the great Orlando Pirates and the even bigger Kaizer Chiefs, and everyone knew that if you played Kaizer Chiefs you would fill your stadium. Kaizer Motaung was a great marketing man who realised he had something everyone wanted.

Arthur Nxumalo, AmaZulu's chairman at the time, convinced me to travel with AmaZulu and flew me to Joburg and the hub of football in South Africa, Soweto. At Orlando Stadium, I asked Arthur why the ground all the way round the bottom of the stands was so wet, as if it had been raining. "If you have your seat for the match and leave to use the toilet," he answered, "you end up forfeiting your place on the stands." So if you needed to relieve yourself, you'd stand up and pee over the top – which made the ground wet and soggy.

This was the South African home of the three teams that caught everyone's eye: Orlando Pirates, Kaizer Chiefs and Moroko Swallows. And the fourth was, of course, AmaZulu. This was also my introduction to football in Soweto and so I decided to throw my lot in with AmaZulu and become their coach.

AmaZulu was the first professional team I coached and the players in our side – Sugar Ray Xulu, Ace Mnikathi, Wellington 'Chippa' Khoza, Richard Ngubane, Eric Ngidi – could stand up to any team, including Kaizer Chiefs. If the Federation had used their brains and been a bit more flexible, they might have controlled football in this country, given the enormous potential football had to attract crowds and money.

Bethwell Masondo, a smart dresser, was the manager of the AmaZulu team that won the League in the 1972/3 season, with Arthur Nxumalo the club chairman and I the coach. AmaZulu were captained by Sugar Ray Xulu and we trained at our facilities just off the Point area surrounded by the harbour.

We were drawn to play Pretoria Callies in the semifinal of the Mainstay Cup at the Orlando Stadium in Soweto, where Chippa Khosa scored a brace to knock out the pretenders to the crown and we moved – deservedly – on to the final.

In 1974 Arthur had signed a new striker from Zululand and, on arriving at our training ground, I found Bethwell sitting on the floor looking disconsolate. When I asked him what was wrong, he said that we were going to lose the final because the signature of the new signing was invalid: the player had never actually been registered. I asked him if anything could be done and his response was that we had to stop the referee from sending in the team sheet and his match report or we'd be disqualified.

Of course, money had to be raised and the word spread like a runaway veld fire. Cash was collected from all over and one night Bethwell was off on his mission. He returned triumphant the next day to a hero's welcome.

I found out later that Bethwell had not only never left kwaMashu and pocketed the money, but he'd made up the entire story to line his pocket.

All was well and we could rightly take our place in the cup final the following day against Orlando Pirates; and as we finished off our training session that Friday afternoon, there was an air of expectancy. The stevedores had been paid and a lot of Castle Lager was being consumed while the famous Smugglers' Inn was filling up.

Our overnight facilities consisted of bunk beds used by schoolchildren and we had to push them together to make them usable for adult footballers. The senior players were always looked after and were afforded the luxury of foam mattresses, but the king was Sugar Ray who not only had first choice of room, but second and third.

That Saturday afternoon a capacity crowd settled in to witness a marvellous game of attacking football. But the game was not without drama. In those days you could only make one substitution. It was nearing the end of the match and we were only just hanging on to our lead. Ace had broken down with a knee injury and everyone was telling me to make another substitute. Of course, I had no way of telling our supporters that we'd already made our one-and-only replacement and would not be allowed to take Ace off the field, so he was left on for nuisance value.

With the score at 2–2, Sugar Ray controlled a pass on the halfway line. His first touch was good before he caressed the ball inside Chiefs' fullback Gerald Dlamini and found Shoes Shamase, the AmaZulu wide player.

I recall saying, "Steady, Shoes, steady," but he did the exact opposite, stopping the ball, then hitting it hard. The ball flew over the Chiefs' goalkeeper … and screamed into the net. AmaZulu had leapt ahead when it mattered most and we went on to win 3–2.

When the final whistle blew and we had beaten Chiefs, the AmaZulu supporters stormed the kwaMashu field and hoisted me high in the air. At the time we dressed in suits because we followed the English game, and as the supporters carried me off the field, they fleeced me and stole my wallet. I learned very, very quickly never to go to another match in a suit. From then on, it was tracksuits.

Some years later, there was a stage when we had the run on Kaizer Chiefs (which hadn't always been the case), and we started a run of outstanding results against them by beating them 3–0 up at Ellis Park, which was a significant outcome for AmaZulu. At the time we had the legendary, giraffe-like figure of Julius Chirwa, who was dominant in that match. Then we played Chiefs in the second round at Kings Park rugby stadium in Durban and went one better. Archie Radebe had come onto the scene and we beat them 5–1. Marks Maponyane scored their goal and Kevin Mudie pulled a hat trick for us. We had dismantled the famous Kaizer Chiefs, and I have a mental picture of Kaizer Motaung slinking away. I had already made my move towards our changing rooms for protection because I knew trouble would follow should the supporters jump the railings into the stadium.

A third match between us was proposed, with a wealthy individual from Tembisa willing to put up the money, but before the game would be played, we had to make a presentation to King Goodwill Zwelithini. We stayed over at the palace and I recall his wife making her way into the room on all fours. Astonished, I asked the king whether she had had an injury, but he answered, "No, that's the custom." David Dlamini, the chairman of AmaZulu by then, lowered himself so that he was below the king's eye level, which was also customary. All I heard was praise singing: "Wena indlovu! Wena indlovu! Bayete! Bayete!" [You are the great bull elephant, we praise you!]

In the match that followed, we gave Chiefs another hiding, beating them at home, with a return match in Joburg to come. It was an extraordinary time for AmaZulu, with us dominating the football scene, certainly in KwaZulu-Natal, up until the late 1980s.

And people still remember. Recently a stranger walked up to me and asked whether I remember those results against Chiefs, when we thumped them three times in a row.

King Goodwill Zwelithini's son played for me at AmaZulu. His Majesty was very loyal to us and we, in turn, paid our respects. One year, prior to the start of the season, we visited him at his palace in order to receive his blessing, an honour that made our supporters very happy. Together with his blessings, the king had invited us to play an exhibition match in Nongoma against an Invitation XI and a prize Nguni bull and cow were on offer to the victors.

At halftime, the magnificent Nguni beasts were paraded alongside the field to be appreciated by the players, spectators and assembled royalty.

Afterwards, we went to King Goodwill's castle, as it was called, where the praise singer honoured all the great Zulu kings – Shaka, Dingaan, Mapandi, Goodwill – and eventually I was given an audience with His Majesty. At the time, I had the Puma agency but noticed the king wore an Adidas tracksuit and footwear. I thought it might seem impertinent and disrespectful for me to comment on his choice of sporting brands.

We had supper at the castle that night and stayed over, before leaving early the next morning. Having beaten the Invitation XI, made up of very enthusiastic young men probably chosen more according to family ties than actual ability, we did offer the cattle to the opposing side as a gesture of goodwill (and, anyway, where would any of us have kept them?), and on accepting the gift, I warned our opponents that bad muti would prevail on the cattle if anything happened to them.

Those cattle probably died of old age, having happily roamed the hills of Nongoma and adding to the numbers of Nguni that are held so sacred in Zulu culture.

In those days, there was a great rivalry between AmaZulu and Kaizer Chiefs, but regular penalties awarded to Chiefs meant that they were frequently ahead of us.

The Iwisa Maize Meal Soccer Spectacular was a competition featuring four teams chosen by telephonic vote so that the teams with the most support generally featured in the season opening competition each year around August. Chiefs were there every year and in 1987 Amazulu managed to attract enough votes to take part.

How it worked was that two teams would play each other in a semifinal, with the final taking place later that afternoon. That year we played Moroka Swallows and beat them, which meant that we would meet Chiefs in the final after they defeated Pirates.

The final saw the mighty uSuthu take the game into extra time. Chiefs led 2–1 before Joel 'The Horse' Faya went on a strong run and smashed the ball powerfully to tie the enthralling encounter 2–2. With time running out, Chiefs were awarded their usual penalty and won 3–2.

The following week was a return match against Chiefs financed by the gentleman from Tembisa in order to give his team an opportunity to beat AmaZulu at least once that season. Close on 30 000 fans packed into Ellis Park Stadium. Chiefs ran into a 3–1 lead, but AmaZulu were determined and fought back and scored two goals to level matters. And then, with time running out – and for the second time in two weeks – Chiefs were awarded another dubious penalty, a penalty that was never a penalty.

I called for the ball and kicked it to their goalkeeper, Gary Bailey, suggesting that if Chiefs needed the cup so badly, they could have it. Then I stomped across Ellis Park – only to be told by Pat Shange and David Tobela of Black Leopards fame to look back at the ensuing mayhem I had unwittingly created. uSuthu supporters had climbed the fence and were storming towards the Chiefs' supporters for an all-out confrontation. During the clash, a fan was shot in the leg. We were rescued by friends and colleagues who escorted us through angry and violent supporters before being ushered into waiting taxis and speeding off straight to the airport. I had to return the following week when the police called me to make a statement; I had been charged with inciting a riot, but nothing ever came of it.

We boarded the plane in the jerseys, shorts and socks we had been wearing for the game, and to this day I have no idea what happened to the clothing we had abandoned back in the changing room. That wooden shield remains in the Amakhosi trophy cabinet, although it really should be returned because Patrick 'Ace' Ntsoelengoe has yet to take the match-winning penalty.

It wasn't all roses off the field either. AmaZulu chairman Arthur Nxumalo was difficult to get hold of, especially around payday, and at one stage the players, represented by Richard Ngubane, Sugar Ray Xulu and Eric Ngidi, threatened not to play if their money was not paid up in full. It was on one such 'non-payment payment' day that I informed Bethwell Masondo, the team manager, that as soon as I had fetched my new car I would pick him up and we would raise the issue of the players' wages with Arthur.

Once I had taken possession of the brand-new Datsun, Bethwell duly directed me to a shortcut to Arthur's Tongaat Trading Store. We travelled on a gravel road through Inanda Hills and then downhill until we arrived at a river that was flowing strongly. I immediately climbed out of the car to inspect the danger, but Bethwell assured me that the river wasn't deep or flowing particularly strong and that we'd manage to drive right through. Of course, the car got stuck. The exhaust, below water level, started spluttering and the car sounded like a speedboat.

A group of boys playing in the river were duly summoned to try to help us out of this mess. By now, I was picturing myself explaining how I had managed to sink my day-old car. Fortunately, with some pushing, shoving, pulling – and a few silent prayers – we managed to get across to the other side. I drove on up the hill towards the trading store, but when we entered, I was informed that the director was unavailable – he had gone to town to pay the players. His car was outside and I swear to this day that I had seen him drop behind the shop counter as we walked in. Payment was nevertheless made and a player revolt averted.

AmaZulu was sponsored by SPAR, a partnership that was hugely valuable to the team – and, given the duration of this association, surely beneficial for SPAR as well – and I am truly grateful for their support over the years.

As part of AmaZulu's support from SPAR, the team was regularly invited to the opening of new stores. Shortly before one of those trips up the KZN North Coast, however, our cocker spaniel Shandy died, which left Madam, our Labrador, without a mate. So I decided to go to the SPCA in Cato Manor and look at what they had. There was this lovely basset hound and everyone in the family wanted him. I enquired about the pup and was told that he was for sale but I would have to return to see whether anyone else was interested in him.

I woke up early and arrived back there at 6am. It was raining, however, and because I didn't want to fall asleep, I got out of the car and walked to the fence, peering over to see if I could see the pup. As I was doing so – and not seeing the little basset anywhere – a cat walked up to me and urinated on my leg. I told myself not to react because they might have cameras around and I'd hardly endear myself to SPCA officials if I did. So I did the right thing and bent down to stroke the cat.

Eight o'clock arrived and I was first in the queue. I presented my credentials and was the very happy recipient of Socks, who I then took home. There was great excitement in the household and everyone, including our neighbours, was delighted.

However, disaster struck when we came home a week later to find Socks missing. We searched high and low, but our dog with the big ears was gone. Forever.

About 25 years later, as the team and I were about to board the bus to return home from the team's trip to open a new SPAR in Empangeni, a gentleman approached me and asked if I still lived in Yellowwood Park – a suburb in Durban where my sons John and Gavin grew up. I explained that we had since moved to Glenwood, but asked why he wanted to know. That's when he confessed that he had stolen our beloved Socks.

I couldn't quite believe what I'd heard and when I asked for proof, he correctly identified the SPCA stamp in Socks's ear. I enquired as to what had happened to Socks and he said that he had taken him to Umlazi.

When I asked why he had done it, he replied, "If I had asked you for the dog, you would not have given him to me." I didn't know how to react. So I phoned Yvonne, John and Gavin and gave them the facts about our missing dog and explained that he had lived very happily for many years. We were all delighted that Socks had done okay. Finally, we had closure.

At one point during my time at AmaZulu we were rolling everybody over and reached the cup final to play Kaizer Chiefs. But just prior to that game, a businessman from Harrismith called to arrange a match between the two sides – which I found very strange, considering we'd be playing them in a couple of weeks. So I called his bluff and suggested that the only way we would play was if he paid a certain amount of money. And, astonishingly, he agreed. Because the venue was some distance away, we had to fly there in two small planes. The players hadn't flown before and weren't very happy about this arrangement, but the plan was to fly in, play the game, collect the money – and it was good, very good, money – and then fly out.

We arrived at Virginia Airport in Durban North, split the team in half because we didn't want all the players in one aircraft, and set off. But as we were about to land, we hit some serious turbulence and both planes began dipping and dropping. The players all turned to me with fear in their eyes, and as we came down to land, the pilot had to abort and pull out, before circling and finally landing safely.

After the match – in which we beat Chiefs, by the way – we returned to the small airport and all the players gravitated toward the pilot with the epaulettes, believing their fate lay in safer hands than that of the pilot of the aborted first landing on the incoming flight. They simply would not get in his plane, despite the fact that he was probably just as experienced as the other pilot. It took a lot of persuading to get the entire team boarded.

Although we enjoyed some success and I had a good relationship with the players, there is always a downside to coaching – aside from losing – and that's having to drop players from the team.

Coaching AmaZulu in the Iwisa Spectacular, I once told Cutter Langa – a huge man, strong as an ox, a good player and competitor – I was leaving him out of the starting line-up. I explained that he had enjoyed a wonderful career at AmaZulu, but his playing days were coming to an end and he wasn't starting that day.

His response was that he simply had to play, a demand I refused to entertain and I explained that I had never been spoken to like this by a player before, but at least he now knew how things stood; the selection was mine alone to make and I refused to be forced into picking anyone.

"Close the door," he said quietly, but firmly, then locked it. "Neither of us is leaving until I've been picked."

Fortunately, someone must have realised what was happening and got us out, narrowly averting a potential crisis. But I never relented and Langa didn't start, although he did end up a good mate of mine. I'm quite sure he thought it would be a good way to go about finishing his career on a high.

Only the side that is picked has any respect for the manager at that point in the process – the rest don't like him much. The guys who come on as substitutes and do well have two thoughts on their minds: that they give the coach one for the road, and that he doesn't leave them out the next time.

That's part and parcel of football.

AmaZulu were always a tough club to handle; the fans were passionate and demanding, but if you could get the team into the top six and play in major cup finals, the supporters would go along with that. I was very fortunate to be involved in a number of cup finals, and even though there was no great success ratio worth boasting about, we did eventually get it right.

AmaZulu were desperate to put one over on the mighty Amakhosi, a team full of inspiring, budding internationals. AmaZulu needed a victory over their arch rivals – there had been numerous attempts, perhaps as many as seven cup finals, only to fail at the final hurdle – and the 1992 Coca-Cola Cup offered the chance.

Chiefs were boosted by the likes of Wade du Plessis, Neil Tovey, Lucas Radebe, Ace Khuse and Gardner Searle, while AmaZulu boasted the hugely talented Joe Mlaba, George Dearnaley, Tim Nzoyi and Steve Baverstock, with the incomparable Shadrack Biemba in goals. In fact, I will never forget Joe's remarkable performance at that 1992 final. Sadly, Joe died of tuberculosis in 2008 at the age of just 40.

But the gamesmanship that came to characterise that game started when Louis Tshakoane flew into town. The Chiefs' PRO thought that the biggest decision of the match would be choosing which way Kaizer Chiefs would face when they received the trophy. But they had not taken into account uSuthu's fighting spirit and skilful ability.

I called Tshakoane's bluff and played mind games of my own, telling him that the team would move out of Durban and into the mountains in Nongoma where we would work with our sangoma. I had consulted with Ian McIntosh, doyen of Natal and later Springbok rugby, to discuss his team's successes on the road. They regularly won away from home, including the historic Natal victory over Northern Transvaal at Loftus Versveld in 1990, and he attributed the team's victories to travelling to the venue a few days before the big match. When Natal (later The Sharks) played rugby matches against Free State in Bloemfontein, they would break the trip to acclimatise to the altitude.

So we at AmaZulu followed suit and booked into the Drakensberg Gardens resort on our way to Johannesburg. Yvonne and I had enjoyed our honeymoon there and it was good to be back and to be able to recall the fond memories we shared there.

There were no real football facilities at the resort but we did manage to arrange a practice match against the local staff on the first day. The second day's preparations were spent running up and down the undulating golf course because I had decided to leave the balls in Durban.

During strategy sessions, I would sit the players down and we would go over and over how we would react when Chiefs got on top during the final. I pointed out that no matter what we thought then, there would be a time – or times – when Chiefs would run at us. I stressed that it was how we reacted in turning bad situations into good ones that would eventually decide who would win the match. We wanted to neutralise Chiefs' strike force and frustrate them – which is good when you're winning, but not so good when you're losing.

When we broke camp, we moved to stay in Harrismith and the players were delighted to be away from bowls, tennis and early nights and now switch on the TVs in their respective hotel rooms. Life was back to normal.

On the Wednesday and Thursday before leaving for Johannesburg, we had a couple of good training sessions with soccer balls. I was content with our preparations and the mental space in which the players found themselves.

That Friday morning we moved on to Johannesburg and in the afternoon had a light training session at Wits' facility. I felt that the players were primed both mentally and physically for the game of our lives. As far as I was concerned, all was well and everything was in place for the big day, but when I followed two or three suspicious-looking players to our Kombi following the training session at Wits, I caught them with some of the famous green stuff. I knocked the stuffing out of them by ordering them out the Kombi and they sheepishly made their way back to the hotel.

I met with Brummie de Leur to discuss what could go wrong on the day. He was a top-class central defender who played for top sides and was a genuine team man, at the time playing for African Wanderers. He was a talented and very big, imposing player who loved a good scrap and he certainly added value to our conversation.

I was grateful once the players arrived safely at the stadium, and once all the hype and singing were behind us, we heard the buzzer signalling that it was time to make our way down the long tunnel onto the beautifully manicured ground now known as FNB Stadium. This is where we would face Chiefs, looking imposing in their gold and black.

AmaZulu controlled the early part of the game and we scored first, just before half-time when George Dearnaley netted one of his many goals that season. Chiefs equalised late in the second half to take the game into extra time. Simon Magagula scored to make it 2–1 and then headed in what would have been his second goal, only to see it disallowed by the referee Trevor Christian. Trevor is very gracious about the mistake he made whenever I see him.

With time running out and Chiefs trailing 2–1, the legendary Lucas Radebe rose majestically to header a cross towards the far post. Only Superman could have saved it, but our own superhero Shadrack Biemba went airborne, stretched his arm, extended his fingers and managed to turn the ball around the corner. What a marvellous save from a marvellous goalkeeper, equal only to André Arendse against Germany's Jürgen Klinsmann for Bafana in 1995.

From the resulting corner, Shadrack gathered the ball and sent it in the direction of the halfway line and AmaZulu countered. The ball found its way to Ephraim Mwelase who steadied himself in the penalty area before unleashing the ball under the body of Wade du Plessis.

With the score 3–1, AmaZulu were home. The Coca-Cola Trophy was ours and I went up to our chairman David Dlamini and hugged him. I also thanked God for the victory. David deserved the trophy, as did Graham O'Connor of SPAR, with whom AmaZulu have enjoyed a long, healthy relationship over the years.

Many years down the line, I still get Chiefs' supporters asking me about our trip to the mountains. I guess only the sangoma and the coach will ever know. Whatever we did, it proved hugely successful.

That game was quite possibly the turning point for the quality of football displayed by AmaZulu. We had won, quite comfortably, against – certainly on paper – the best team outside of the Bush Bucks side I coached in 1985.

One of the features of this great contest was the battle between Rudolph Seale and Joe Mlaba, as was the emergence of George Dearnaley as a top-class player.

With 20 league goals, George was the 1992 NSL Golden Boot winner and was later capped at International level for South Africa. He was playing college football in America in late 1991, when his dad and I bumped into each other at the local SPAR in Yellowwood Park where we both lived.

I asked George Senior after his son, and told him that I would be coaching AmaZulu again the following year and that South Africa were being readmitted to FIFA, which held obvious promise for aspiring players. His father passed the information on and within a week George was back in South Africa.

"My dream to play pro football and represent my country was on its way to being a reality," George admits. "The 1992 and 1993 seasons were probably the best AmaZulu ever had. We won the league in 1972, but outside of that hadn't won anything else since. Twenty years later, with Clive as our coach, we won the Coca-Cola Cup, beating Chiefs in the final, and the following year came third in the league behind Sundowns and Swallows, but above Chiefs and Pirates.

"Those were two great seasons."

Bafana Bafana celebrations in the change room after the AFCON final 1996, Soweto, Johannesburg.

SEVEN

Black and White

"He was always very good at mixing cultures. He didn't so much integrate as welcome different cultures into his teams."
— CARL PETERS

Because football wasn't going to be dictated to by the government about what they could do, they challenged the laws of this country well before the politicians. Certainly my travels into the townships were not part of the government's grand plan to keep South Africans 'living apart'.

At one stage, a team from the UK was invited to play against local clubs in South Africa, but AZAPO stepped in and refused to allow it to happen. Kaizer Motaung agreed and the tour was cancelled. It was a case of 'no normal sport in an abnormal society'.

In the 1970s and 1980s, in particular, South Africa was in a very confused state. A multiracial team would travel to Joburg but only white members would be given rooms in a hotel. If we played in Umtata, it was the opposite.

Sugar Ray Xulu, an outstanding footballer and an equally outstanding person, was the one who took me into the townships, introducing me to what should be happening in South African football at the time. This was an opportunity to wear your rosette and argue the merits of whether the country should be governed by the white National Party or a black majority government. I think I was a bit of a coward, because I tended to sit on the fence.

When I first started becoming politically vocal, I asked the candidate for the Herstigte Nasionale Party – a white conservative to moderately right-wing political party that no longer exists – why I had the vote but a wonderful human being like Sugar Ray Xulu did not. After it all got a little heated and I started shouting "Free Mandela!" – in anger and to rile up the conservative middle-aged man in khaki – a police officer walked across to us and suggested we don't spoil the special day that was the local election, that what I was saying wasn't right. He added that, should I continue with my behaviour and not leave, he would forcibly remove me and lock me up.

Politically and socially, these were volatile times in the immensely fractured South Africa. But playing in the townships remained a wonderful experience for me and I never once felt threatened. Fans and supporters were filling the stadiums, and they knew I was there purely and simply to coach football. I'd drive through townships in KZN, Bloemfontein, Kimberley and Joburg, and the ululating, waving and smiling locals would prove to me that I was accepted, even loved. It made my heart sing.

Many interesting times lay ahead for our political landscape, and although it would take many years and plenty of dark days for changes to be made, statements were already being heard on sports fields. The movement for change was strong and football – the area in which I was actively involved – broke down more barriers than anything else.

I recall going to the Tropicale, a favourite Durban haunt. It has since closed, but I would guess many Durbanites will remember their milkshakes and black forest cake. Sometimes, families would remain in their cars and order meals that were placed on trays and clipped onto the car windows. The Tropicale was truly an institution in Durban.

One day, on the way to a coaching session in the townships, I took Sugar Ray Xulu there. I was amazed at Sugar Ray's popularity in the townships; he was a real legend wherever he went. I would see the adulation in the children's eyes as they ran up to the car, and then they would run away when they saw me, a white man. Perhaps I represented something they feared and didn't want to see.

With Sugar Ray in the passenger seat next to me in the parking lot of the Tropicale, we asked the waiter for two milkshakes, but you could see the consternation in his eyes. He couldn't serve Sugar in a normal glass, he said, but he could give him a paper cup and I would get the glass. This can't be happening, I thought to myself. And when the waiter returned, I handed Sugar the glass and took the paper cup. What a crazy time in our country's history.

Two worlds existed in South Africa, and the 1970s and '80s was a dark time, especially if you were black. Everything was messed up. I couldn't even drink out of the same cup as someone like Sugar Ray Xulu, who was a much better person than I could ever have been.

There were so many injustices. One incident that I'm not very proud of explains just how shortsighted and prejudiced people could be … AmaZulu had played Orlando Pirates and I had made a request to the police at Orlando Stadium to escort us to the airport after our match, because if we had to do it on our own steam, we'd miss our flight back home. Although they wouldn't provide the escort, they did contact the airport, warning them that we would be cutting things a bit fine.

In those days, you filled the stadium, and as players tend to do – especially after they've won – they took their time after the match. So I took all their identity documents with me to the airport and ran ahead to the check-in counter. I explained to the very officious lady behind the counter that the players wouldn't be long, and that I was there to check everyone in the team in on their behalf.

She refused. She said she would not let the players on until they were all together, in front of her counter. I tried to get her to change her mind, explaining I had been dropped off specifically to facilitate the team's boarding passes and seat allocations. But she just shook her head. I explained that we didn't have the money to stay the night in Joburg. What would she want us to do, I asked. Where should we stay the night?

She insisted that it wasn't her problem. I then retorted that had we been the Northern Transvaal rugby team, she would be taking good care us, but because we were a black team, she wouldn't help in the slightest.

I was irked and, foolishly, phoned Yvonne to tell her I wasn't coming home and that we'd have to stay in Joburg for the night. Then as the airline official made her way towards me I told Yvonne, "Here comes the stupid bitch!" – which was completely wrong of me and I can't apologise more for my outburst, but emotions were riding high.

I was charged for my behaviour. Raymond Hack of SAFA told me to go home and that everything would be sorted out on Monday, which it was. Incidents such as these were common, especially if you were black and on the receiving end, but I regret my words. I can't deny that my temper was frayed.

There was a lot of rivalry between football teams in the 1980s and it wasn't just one club against another, but very much along racial lines. When we went to Soweto with Durban City, you'd be spat at through the fence as you ran onto the field, for no other reason than Durban City reflected what was happening in South African society.

Kaizer Chiefs represented black South Africa, so every time the teams met we were essentially going to war. It was White vs Black – an echo of apartheid society that existed at the time. It became even more commonplace when Swallows and Pirates emerged as real powers on the local football scene, so it was a huge ask to go into different townships and win.

Fortunately, I was accepted within the football fraternity and that made my job a lot easier. The only times it was difficult was when we booked into hotels and the receptionist would rush off to call the manager, who would come out, see that there were blacks in the party and immediately point out that blacks were not allowed in the hotel. We'd then move into central Joburg – not far from Hillbrow – which seemed to be a lot more liberal, and find accommodation there. In fact, I remember twice lining up at reception, assigning the players to their various rooms, and then asking for my key, only to be told that no whites were allowed to stay there.

It's funny looking back now, but not so much then, in the bitter winter of places like Kimberley, and being on the other side of racial intolerance and the craziness of the Group Areas Act.

At one time I had the dual role of coaching Juventus and AmaZulu, one amateur and one professional club. Juventus had played in Pietermaritzburg on the Saturday afternoon and then we drove up during the night to Kimberley, where AmaZulu was taking on Dalton Brothers on Sunday.

It was in the middle of winter, and we arrived at the hotel some distance out of town and, at about two o'clock in the morning, I booked everyone into their rooms before asking for my key. The manager on duty said, "Sorry, no whites are allowed here … You'll have to drive back into town." I doubted that there would be too many places open to accommodate a guest at two in the morning, so I climbed into my car, drove up the road, did up the windows and tried to sleep. A car is not the most comfortable place to get some rest, especially when there are no pillows or blankets for comfort and warmth in the dead of winter. I doubt I got more than an hour or two's sleep.

At about 6am in the morning, cold, cramped and with a serious sense of humour failure, I couldn't take it any more and drove back to the hotel. I asked the hotel guard if he'd let me into the grounds. He refused. Eventually, after much pleading, I handed over a few rand and that seemed to produce the right kind of magic. I managed to get in and have a hot shower and then drove into town to have some breakfast. I met up with the team on the Sunday morning, but it was not the most comfortable trip I ever made as a football coach.

Durban City hosted what must have been the first multiracial camp, known as 'A Kick in the Grass'. The plan was to hold it at Kingsmead cricket ground, but the government stopped us, refusing to allow us to use government property. Then Roger Gardner from the Natal Rugby Union gave us permission to use the Kings Park rugby ground and the first black kid who signed up was Joe Mlaba, who arrived at the camp with his boots in a plastic bag – he didn't even have a sleeping bag. Joe, who was simply incredible for AmaZulu in the Coca-Cola Cup final when we defeated Kaizer Chiefs 3–1, ended up playing for Bafana Bafana.

While at Durban City, it became clear, however, that not all sporting teams were equal. The Natal cricket team had everything: sandwiches before they went on, a choice of three meals at lunch, scones with jam and cream at tea time, and piping hot toasted sandwiches – with a couple of beers thrown in – at the end of the day's play. I thought to myself, a little angrily, that the footballers' training grounds just down the road had none of those luxuries, not even a toilet in sight; the nearest tree served that purpose.

The sacrifices footballers made were huge.

After winning the league, AmaZulu were invited to play in the Champion of Champions tournament and came up against Kaizer Chiefs in Soweto in front of something like 64 000 spectators. We had flown up to Joburg, booked into our hotel, had our pre-match meal and then driven to Soweto. There were as many people outside the venue as there were inside and we had to get through them. We had to park more than a kilometre away and when we finally reached the stadium and made our way to our changing rooms, we discovered that they had doctored it with muti. It stank to high heavens, so – no problem – we just changed in the corridor. We lost 3–2.

One of the incidents that stands out most in my mind was when we were playing a double-header in and around Joburg. Rodney Charles and Arno Wood were coloured players in our team, and when we arrived at the hotel in Klerksdorp that evening after the second match, the manager looked at us and said, "Sorry, you can't stay here." So the whole team decided we would leave and drive all the way back to the Johannesburger Hotel where we would be accepted.

Clive came from a background of coaching AmaZulu and,

playing in townships with him, it came down to respect: respect for other cultures. So when South Africa went through this incredible change and became a democratic country, it was nothing new for Bafana.

Football didn't emerge at the same time as the Rainbow Nation; it had already embraced all the colours of the rainbow way back in the 1970s as a professional league with mixed teams. Within football circles, we didn't distinguish between black, white, coloured or Indian – we were simply footballers.

When it came to Bafana under Clive, you could say we had probably the most mixed team possible. That blend was our strength; the diversity in our culture was hugely important. We were fortunate that we'd had a taste of this diversity for a long time – it wasn't something new to us. I didn't suddenly meet and start playing with a black man in the same team and Clive, too, had been a part of integrated cultures for many years.

Clive enhanced the diversity and the team respected him for that. He wasn't a white man coming from overseas to coach this national team. The players, regardless of race, respected Clive's sense of unity. And because of this, there was never any comment about a white captain and a white coach. There was never a question about the racial make-up of the team. When you're successful, no one can question it.

The togetherness we had, as a team, could never be denied.

As much as we were victorious on that day of the Africa Cup of Nations final, if Bafana had been an all-black or all-white team, we would have lost the impact we eventually had.

A mixed team enjoying the successes we did was a symbol of what the country could achieve and become. If a football team represented different cultures working together for a common goal, and succeeding, why could South Africa not succeed? A football team represents a country: you need heroes and leaders, people who are looked up to and respected, and we had that in 1996.

– Neil Tovey

As far as the racial make-up of the team went, there was balance – "which couldn't have been easy at the time," says Emy Casaletti-Bwalya, whose association with the national team through apparel sponsor Kappa was a very successful and mutually beneficial one. "It was never an issue that there was a white coach and white captain, and that has a lot to do with Clive's personality. He was the coach, not a white coach, just a very popular one."

After we won the Africa Cup of Nations, a bunch of friends and I would walk and run along the beachfront, and I remember once starting out at Addington Hospital where people of all shapes, sizes and colours joined us. Although many started to toyi-toyi in jubilation, it reached a stage where it felt quite threatening – the crowd was huge. I suggested to Henry Naudé and Charlie White that we duck into a restaurant – Butcher Boys, I think – to escape the throng. I asked the owner Allan Lazarus if we could hide and he took us to his office for safety. The crowd was going crazy around the front of the restaurant and we were able to eventually duck out the back and make our way down the street.

It could get pretty hair-raising, even if the vibe was excited and friendly, because big numbers are difficult to control.

Clive famously spits water on the field as an umuthi sign to the crowd, indicating that a goal is coming soon, during a World Cup qualifier in 1997.

EIGHT

uMuthi

*"The umuthi was strong if you won. If you lost, you
were just a bad player."*
– George Dearnaley

Magic. Sorcery. Witchcraft. Wizardry. Whatever you choose
to call it, umuthi – or traditional medicine – has been an
integral part of African beliefs and cultural practice for
decades, even influencing the outcomes of football matches.

With such a divergent path between black and white footballing
structures, traditional customs took on an important role in black
football, particularly in the rituals and potions designed to enhance
the team's play and improve the chances of success, as well as to
intimidate the opposition.

The sangoma – traditional healer or diviner – attached to a
team gives the players the extra edge that coaching, preparation,
skill and ability cannot provide to win games. In all the teams, the
main player would always be the sangoma. When he is having a
successful run, he earns the most – by far; more than the coach
even. Like players' agents today, he earns a lot of money, happily
taking his pay for arranging the outcomes of games in our favour.
But, like the coach, he is just as vulnerable when it comes to how

much success and failure will influence his career.

The psychology behind traditional beliefs is also very interesting, because although the sangoma is highly regarded, feared even, everyone also prays before a match, sometimes even two or three times. So there is no question that most players practise Christianity and pray to God. But they recognise, too, that it's not a bad thing to also go along with the sangoma, because if his magic can help them win a game, then everyone is happy.

The sangoma has always played a significant role – and still does – but as a white man it took some getting used to the traditional practices.

Whatever the sangoma cooked in his Primus stove looked to me like a dead meercat, and when we were on the road, staying in various hotels, the smoke from whatever was being cooked would often set off the fire alarms. Then everyone would have to explain why there were logs and other unidentifiable objects floating around in the bath.

In my first year with AmaZulu in 1974, the club made it through to the cup final where we met the mighty Orlando Pirates. Our club's chairman, Arthur Nxumalo, decided that, for the first time, he would fly rather than drive us up to Joburg and we all rolled up at the airport resplendent in our new blazers and flannels and looking like the smartest team in the world. When we arrived at the hotel, Arthur said to me: "You won't lose this cup final." I asked him how he could be so sure, and he put his hand in his pocket and brought out an empty Vaseline bottle containing a piece of string, tied 11 times. The sangoma he had visited during the week had given it to him, and had informed him that we needed to visit a certain place in the ground, where we would discover the umuthi that the Pirates' sangoma was employing to stop us from winning.

"We can't lose because of this," said Arthur. "We dug it up in kwaMashu, near our home ground." My response was that the sangoma must have put it there a couple of days previously, that it could hardly be so coincidental. But Arthur argued that it was the real thing, insisting that the final was all sorted.

We were staying at the Diplomat Hotel in Johannesburg and

everyone wanted to have a role to play in our success. The next thing, these big Cadillacs arrived to pick us up. On the way to the stadium, Arthur dropped the bombshell that we had to stop off in Hillbrow first. I knew, of course, that there would be signs of 'No Blacks Allowed' all over the place and, desperate to avoid trouble and even prison, I protested to Arthur that we simply had to get to the ground and warm the players up; we had so much to do. He begged, determined to finish what he had started and, with that, the front vehicle veered off the route to towards Hillbrow.

In those segregated days, when black people weren't allowed to use the lifts and had to enter round the back, we were forced to climb about 10 flights of stairs up the fire escape, which is far from ideal just before a cup final match. At the top we were met by a wizened old man dressed in his finest sangoma regalia.

He took out his porcupine quill and proceeded to poke all the players. Then, with the players standing in a line, waiting their turn, he cut their ankles with a blade to draw blood, presumably to influence their footwork on the field.

But there was one player who would never agree to this kind of thing, the hugely talented Richard Ngubane, who should have played overseas. At times, he would come to me, knowing he was our best player, and say, "I can't play today." I would ask why and he would explain that he had no boots. Arthur would immediately respond by taking Richard to the local sports shop and buying him the best boots available; Richard knew the best make of Adidas or Puma, and Arthur would buy a few pairs, knowing this would stand him in good stead with Richard for the next season.

On the occasion of the final and the visit to the sangoma, when it was Richard's turn to be cut with the blade, he turned around and said, "There's no way I'm having it done." What proceeded was a confrontation between the two, but Richard's obstinacy won and he refused to take part.

The drama didn't end there.

When we arrived at Orlando Stadium, the full-house signs were up and no one was allowed to enter the ground. So there we were, changing in the dust at a school next door, the players' boots dirtied as we warmed up around people selling all manner of local brews and shisa nyama (braaied meat) of indeterminate body parts. The carnival atmosphere was electric.

On being denied access to the stadium, club chairman Arthur Nxumalo explained to the guards that he had to get AmaZulu into the changing room and the officials pointed to a ladder that we needed to climb to enter the stadium. Arthur climbed the ladder and was met by three policemen in the old uniforms, insisting that he was chairman of the club and needed to bring his team in. They argued back and forth until it got to a stage where they insisted he pay for us. So he did.

Although Arthur had had to pay to watch his own team play, we managed to play in a wonderful cup final, the start of wonderful things for AmaZulu. Shakes Mashaba and Jomo Sono were in that outstanding Pirates team and, although it was a very even affair, Jomo hit a shot that bounced awkwardly in front of Fred 'The Cat' Mfeka, hit his shoulder and bounced in.

We got beaten 1–0 and the angry sangoma was quick to point out that Richard Ngubane's refusal to be pricked with the porcupine quill was the very reason we lost. He insisted that Richard had weakened the chain and had cost us the final.

At one stage, when we beat Kaizer Chiefs three times in one season, defeating them 3–1, 5–1 and 2–1, the highest paid player in the team was our sangoma, who was loving every minute of it. He stayed with AmaZulu for a very long time.

When we beat Kaizer Chiefs in the cup final, they asked me whether I had gone "into the mountains". I told them I had gone to Nongoma, because that's where the sangoma is. I didn't tell them where I really went because that would have ruined the spice of the story.

In 1987, Sy Lerman, the doyen of sports writers, was finalising the nominees for the Footballer of the Year award. He got hold of me and confided that our captain and top player, Archie Radebe, had enjoyed an excellent season and if he performed that weekend in the Mainstay Cup Final against Kaizer Chiefs – and if we won – he would be looked upon favourably for the award. The prize was R50 000, which was a lot of money at the time.

The team flew into Johannesburg confident, in the right frame of mind, and took the game to Chiefs.

We dominated but got caught out with a long pass down the middle. Marks Maponyane touched the ball past our advancing goalkeeper, Derek Naidoo, and Chiefs were in front. With time running out, Chiefs' Jackie Masike passed the ball back to his keeper, Banks Setlhodi, a poor pass that Archie read perfectly, intercepting it and latching on to the ball. As he moved into the 18-yard area, he went one-on-one with the keeper and waltzed around him, leaving him flat-footed and on the ground.

With no one between himself and the empty goal, Archie could really just have walked the ball into the back of the net. "Steady, Archie," I said to myself. "Just take your time," and that's exactly what he did. Perfectly. I had already started celebrating when Archie did the impossible, playing the ball into the side netting.

It must be the most horrible miss of all time, certainly Jomo Sono, the presenter that evening, called it the Miss of the Century.

In the changing room afterwards, I eventually summoned the courage to ask our disconsolate and completely shattered captain what had happened. He replied that he had spotted that mischievous little troublemaker, the Tokoloshe, running next to him and that had put him off. Archie died in 2015 holding on to that belief.

I had to tell Archie the sad news that he had lost out on the Footballer of the Year award. Not only had he lost the club a bonus and the honour of winning the Mainstay Cup, but also the R50 000 prize he would have won with that award.

Just a couple of days before that cup final, I had come to training to find all the players were sitting on the ground, including Archie, the captain and spokesman; they wanted more money. I explained that the chairman wasn't able to give them more than the prize money; why did they want more? They said they were unhappy with the bonus structure, that they had reached the semifinal, had been paid one amount, but that there was a secondary amount outstanding, and until they received it, they refused to train. I got them to train on the basis that I would speak to David Dlamini that evening, but I also explained that they had been paid the entire bonus offered to them. They insisted, though, that they had been promised a second bonus by David.

With all the hype around the big match, I asked David what he was going to do about it. He turned around and said: "This is what we're going to do about it: we're going to pay them."

And that's what happened: they were paid and returned to training voluntarily, wallets and bank balances bulging a little more than before.

I confronted Jimmy Ormshaw, the youngest player in the group (knowing that it wouldn't be worth asking a senior player, who would deny it), and asked him if it was true that they had been offered extra money. He didn't know where to look. He was sheepish, eyes on the ground, and eventually revealed that David Dlamini had indeed promised them the extra bonus, that it wasn't a case of the players getting greedy; all they wanted was what had been promised to them.

The sad part about it was that they were punished. They should have gone home with an extra R50 000; Archie had lost a great opportunity. After his brush with the Tokoloshe, I'm not quite sure if he ever really recovered as a player again.

Maybe David Dlamini got his payback; I still don't know.

"During our AmaZulu days, we didn't see much of Clive when the muti was around; he would always be there, mind you, but certainly on the outside," Neil Tovey explains. "But he would reluctantly come in now and then. He understood that you have to respect cultures and, whether he liked it or not, he knew that he couldn't move away from it. If it was part of the culture of the team, you would do it, as long as it fitted in with team needs. If a goat's throat needed to be cut, then they had to respect when it would be done. He wouldn't actually run away; he'd be there, but not for very long."

I got quite close to George Dearnaley because we would travel home together after football training sessions. I'd give him a lift as we lived in the same area and we'd chat on the way home to Yellowwood Park. He once raised the issue of muti with me and I explained to him that my attitude was that this was their team and their culture; we were on the outside and needed to adapt. We didn't have to believe in it, but we had to respect it. Those of us who weren't Zulu adjusted to the notion of umuthi, such as imphepho – herbs and leaves that are burnt, so that the smoke in the changing room would make you more powerful on the field. When we were playing away from home and staying in a hotel, the sangoma would prepare something in the team manager's bath water – things floating around and the water discoloured – and all the players would have to bath in it.

"It smelled disgusting, but we all did it," Dearnaley recalls. "Steve Baverstock and I had a pact that we would never swallow anything that we couldn't identify and every now and then a plastic cup with one or two things floating on the top would be passed around and we'd put our lips to it but never take a sip."

The attitude was that this was a Zulu club and we respected that the players believed in the power of umuthi.

Our famous trip to play Kaizer Chiefs in the Coca-Cola Cup final in front of 60 000 people at Soccer City was a classic example of the role played by superstition. We spent a few days travelling to Johannesburg, stopping in Harrismith, then the Drakensberg and so on; it was all about acclimatising to the altitude. On the way, in the middle of nowhere, one of the two minivans hit a goat and killed it. There was huge debate about what we were going to do with the body.

"Some said we had to take it with us to Joburg, while Clive was doing his head, telling us we couldn't take it in the minivan with us," Dearnaley explains. "After about an hour of haggling and arguing about the fate of the goat, someone suggested we take it to the local village and present it to them as a gift."

So it was that the whole AmaZulu team arrived at a small village of mud huts, the headman came out to greet us and we presented the goat to him, as well as R100 in payment for the dead animal. The whole village gave us their blessing and off we went.

We won the Coca-Cola Cup and after the game the players insisted it was because of the goat.

But the sangoma, who doubled as our security guy, had given two players something in their hands and a couple of instructions, and we were told, as a team, that nobody was allowed to cross the halfway line until those two players had done their thing in Chiefs' half and returned to our half.

So Chiefs kick off, the ball goes back from Shane McGregor to Ace Khuse who looks up and there are two of our players sprinting past him, neither of them even glancing in his direction as they head towards the 18-yard area, sprinkle whatever was given to them by the witchdoctor on the ground, then sprint back to our half.

Only once they were back in our half did we start playing. All the AmaZulu fans were celebrating in the knowledge that there was a mysterious but beneficial force at play, while you could hear a murmur of bewilderment from the Chiefs' fans. We ended up winning 3-1, two scored in that particular goal.

In one match against Moroka Swallows in Durban, we had one guy who came with two little pieces of wood, to put one in each of my boots. But during the warm-up, these pieces of wood were irritating me, so I went to the bathroom and flushed them down the toilet and thought nothing more of it.

We smashed Swallows 4-1, I scored two goals and after-wards the guy was all over me. Two pieces of wood, two goals, he was the man. Next time, he promised me, I was getting three pieces of wood!

– George Dearnaley, striker (AmaZulu and Bafana Bafana)

We had one dodgy guy who decided he would be our next 'muti man' and came in for a game against Moroka Swallows at Ellis Park.

He was dressed in a black flowing robe, and looked seriously scary. He had a candle burning in the middle of the changing room and what looked like blood on the floor around it. We all stood in a circle around it and he started chanting at a million miles an hour. One of the players next to me started shivering – you could sense that he was terrified. Then, at the end of his five-minute incantation, the sangoma said in the deepest voice: "From now on, AmaZulu will never lose another match."

The players were all pumped up, ready for the game, ready to win and made their way down the long passage towards the field in high spirits and full of energy. The game started and they were on fire, playing in an all-white kit, like Real Madrid. Within 10 minutes, AmaZulu were 1–0 up thanks to a fantastic goal from Simon Magagula.

AmaZulu had a strong following up in Joburg, with many fans coming from the mines and we had 5000 supporters going off their heads. After the goal was scored, the sangoma ran across the field towards the halfway line, arms open like he's doing the aeroplane run that I enjoyed doing and the fans erupted even further.

But that was the beginning of the end for us in that match. We were annihilated, losing 4–1. Our muti man disappeared even before the end of the match and we never saw the guy again.

Clive knew the power of the mind and wasn't afraid to use it to good effect.

In 1992, we played Chiefs in Durban and one of our players, nicknamed Ninja, had a clash of heads with one of the Chiefs players and went down hard. There was blood all over the place and with only a few minutes left to play and holding on to our lead, there were no more substitutions available for us so he couldn't leave the field.

It was a scorching hot day and although he was the coach, Clive was also sometimes the medicine guy and he ran on with a bottle of water and a tub of Vaseline. He pours water over Ninja's head, slathers great handfuls of Vaseline all over the cut, shouting at him in Zulu: "Hhayi esaba, Hhayi esaba"

[Don't be afraid, don't be a coward], adding, "Your ancestors are watching you" and suddenly the eyes roll back into place, he jumps up like nothing is wrong and continues playing. We even managed to score a third goal.

After the game, he collapsed from loss of blood and passed out.

– George Dearnaley

Clive gives one of his inspirational team talks to Shaun Bartlett,
Mark Fish and Lucas Radebe during AFCON 1996.
(Matthew Ashton/PA Images)

NINE

Bafana Bafana

"Clive came in, listened to our concerns and immediately fixed the little things. That showed in our success."
– NEIL TOVEY

I n early 1994, I received a call from Kaizer Motaung, who wanted to meet with me. We'd had a long association and knew each other well, and I certainly liked him. I suppose I was the right candidate at the time and he probably trusted me. I'd won the league with Durban City, and Bush Bucks and AmaZulu had been runners-up. There had also been seven or eight major cup finals over the years – the majority of which had been against Kaizer Chiefs. The win ratio was terrible, though – I'd lost just about every final.

There was an element of revenge, however, when AmaZulu beat Chiefs 3–1 to be crowned South African League Cup Champions in 1992. Towards the end of my club career, things began to turn around. By then we had won three national cup finals and one second-division cup final, and had featured in nine or 10 cup finals.

So when Kaizer and I met at Kings Park, I thought he wanted to speak to me about signing George Dearnaley. Instead, he said that he would like me to take the national team coaching job. I was given a deadline of the following day to make my decision. I then flew up to Joburg to meet Stix Morewa and Molefi Oliphant at the airport hotel and there they asked me to take over coaching the team from Augusto Palacios, who had been at the helm between 1992 and 1994.

When they asked for my terms, I told them I wanted R12 500 per month (when Brazilian Carlos Parreira coached Bafana, he received R1.7 million a month and, looking back at that, I truly think my wife married the wrong guy). They said they would come back to me with an answer and within days I received a call from Stix Morewa informing me that I was the new coach. I was delighted. I went home and might have had a glass of wine or champagne, I don't recall, but we certainly had something to celebrate the good news.

I was appointed in 1994, with two years to plan for the 1996 Africa Cup of Nations. At that stage, the team was referred to as the Four-by-Fours (or 4x4s), having taken a couple of smacks down the line, losing 4–1 to Zimbabwe, 4–0 to Nigeria and 4–0 to Mexico.

When he became national team coach, I sat down with him and we had a discussion around where I felt things were going wrong with Bafana at that stage. One of the aspects I touched on was that Bafana Bafana felt alienated, it was us as the team, and then there was the SAFA hierarchy and we needed to bring that closer together. And that's what Clive did.

Then within the team there were Chiefs players and Pirates players and because we were still new at this, the problems of past rivalries remained. There were these different elements that we had to investigate and fix. One thing I also spoke to Clive about was the kit we were issued with when we went to camp. We'd collect our tracksuits and training kit and then return it all after the camp. We'd ask the question, were we really playing for our national team? Then in the course of playing for your club, you'd see people walking around in SAFA gear and think, they've got all this kit and yet we who play for our country get nothing to show for it.

It was these little things that irked us and I told Clive that, but added that this was a good team and just little changes needed to be made. I didn't have to tell him that it was about making the players feel more valued because I knew he would fix that and ensure that those small components needing change would be changed.

He did this immediately and it showed in our success. He was open to listening to our concerns, not once asserting himself as a coach who was the boss and wouldn't listen to input from the players, or act on it. He encouraged these conversations and more. We had fun together, we joked and when it was time to raise issues, not only the captain spoke, the whole team contributed.

- Neil Tovey

When I took over as Bafana Bafana coach, my first action was to find out why Neil Tovey had been sacked as captain of the national team. The story I had heard was that Neil and some of the players had gone to Ellis Park to watch a game and the team doctor, also there, reported that the players had been drinking. As many good footballers will testify, one beer always turns into two, and two into three and so on, and Neil had been called into a meeting and relieved of his captaincy. When I discussed this with Neil, he was adamant that he had drunk no more than one beer and although Steve Komphela, an eloquent, charming man, was the captain at the time and had done nothing wrong, I decided to return the captaincy to Neil.

When I had first encountered Neil and his massive feet at a Juventus training session, I had shaken his outstretched hand and been impressed with the presence he had about him. His brother Mark was a super player who had been denied the opportunity of playing international football because of South Africa's sporting isolation. Mark was the best central defender I had worked with: quick, well balanced, with a good football brain, while Neil was different. Neil played in the middle, passed the ball better than most and was a great team man. It was a privilege to work with someone with such a fantastic work ethic. Overall, both brothers were a credit to the game.

When I reinstated Neil as captain, I watched as he would walk into the breakfast room, approach the players and give each one a hug, enquiring how they and their families were and making each player feel important. I think that alone showed that the right decision about his position in the team had been made.

Two years before the 1996 Africa Cup of Nations, Yvonne accompanied me to Tunis, the beautiful capital of Tunisia where the 1994 tournament was taking place. Because South Africa was no longer the pariah state and had finally been reunited with the world, particularly in the sporting arena, I was afforded plenty of attention.

It was after this trip that Yvonne suggested I make no foolish statements, and I assured her I wouldn't.

I was being interviewed by Emmanuel Maradas, the editor of *African Soccer* magazine, a hugely popular publication well received across the continent. With South Africa's previous sporting isolation, I gathered that there might be a feeling of animosity towards us and although I said all the right things during the interview, I was finally asked how I thought Bafana would fare if they were playing in this tournament (remember, we were referred to as the Four-by-Fours at this point).

In response, I suggested that Bafana would win the next AFCON tournament (in 1996) and then qualify for the World Cup to be held in France in 1998. This caused quite a stir and I realised that I had put my foot right in it. Who was I to make such lofty utterances to the rest of Africa?

Sometimes, as a leader, you say these things to motivate yourself, the team and the supporters. Me and my big mouth.

But fate was good to me and Bafana achieved with both class and panache.

In the December just before the Africa Cup of Nations, I thought I'd test the waters, and invite Germany to come out and play us. Remember, too, there was the Sean Dundee affair at the time – did he want to belong to South Africa or Germany?

During the build-up to the AFCON tournament, there was a debate regarding the selection of Durban-born Dundee. I first met him when he was playing for Bayview, a popular amateur club based on the Bluff coached by Gordon Igesund. The two struck up a very strong bond once Gordon helped kick-start Sean's football career.

Gordon advised Sean to further his career by moving overseas and joining German club Stuttgarter Kickers. He soon became flavour of the month and South Africa became very excited at the prospect of a local star making it big abroad. I saw Sean as the final jigsaw piece in the puzzle, to form a fantastic strike force with Philemon Masinga, Shaun Bartlett and Mark Williams.

All four were gaining international experience at club level, Philemon with Leeds and then Bari in Italy, Shaun with Charlton in England, and Mark with Wolves, also in England. With Sean Dundee playing in the German leagues, I could complete the quartet.

They were all tall in stature, strong, quick and brave; it all looked very promising.

I regularly invited Sean to join the Bafana Bafana squad, but he turned me down each time and seemed more interested in developing his club career than endorsing his international selection.

So I asked SAFA to invite Germany to play us in a friendly match in Johannesburg six weeks before the Africa Cup of Nations tournament and, to my surprise, I received a call to say that Sean wanted to join the squad. I thought long and hard about it before including him in the Bafana Bafana setup and, once he arrived, he soon settled into the team training. He later intimated that he felt ostracised, although he never showed it at the time.

On the Thursday, we boarded the bus for a training session and Sean asked if his team coach could travel with us. I agreed, and also suggested that he bring his family with, just to endorse our sincerity, especially as it would make him feel more comfortable and at ease.

The rest is pure speculation.

Sean and his coach spent the trip to the training ground in deep conversation; I believe they were discussing the possibility that he might be offered the very tempting proposition of representing Germany instead of Bafana Bafana.

During practice, Sean went down with a calf muscle injury and David Becker, our physiotherapist, made the decision to withdraw him. I have no doubt that this was an orchestrated move and my feelings have been well documented. Sean's club coach must have informed him of Berti Vogts's intention to select him and I had a go at the German coach publically about this.

To this day, Sean has never properly discussed what really transpired. Suffice to say, the South African press had a field day lambasting the German Federation, Berti Vogts, the club coach, Sean and myself.

The sad thing is that Bafana Bafana ended up being short-changed and Sean lost out on a golden opportunity to represent his country. After switching nationality, he did go on to make one appearance for Germany B in 2000, scoring in that match against Russia.

That fixture against Germany was a calculated risk, but we had remained unbeaten for 12 matches until then and wanted to see how far down the line we were. When they arrived, everyone who was anyone in the football world climbed off the luxury bus, including the likes of Andreas Möller and Jürgen Klinsmann and their team-mates, all perfectly and professionally attired. This prompted Mark Williams to suggest we just pack up and go home.

I bore this in mind and when I gave my pre-match talk to the players, I left Doctor Khumalo to last and said to him: "You have to ignite this crowd, because we need them on our side; only our mothers, grandmothers, wives and girlfriends believe we can win this match … The Germans believe they are unstoppable and you need to turn on the magic."

The stadium was filled to capacity and early on in the game the ball trickled towards our bench. As Möller came to close Doc down, he stuck the ball straight through the German's legs and, with that, the crowd went absolutely wild. The stadium erupted and we never looked back. This was the African flair that everyone spoke about and Doctor had accepted the challenge. That night he was on fire. In the last few minutes of the game, deadlocked 0–0, he went on a diagonal run into the box, drawing the defenders with him and then back-heeled the ball to Zane Moosa, who was hovering around the 18-yard area. Zane hit it well – very well – but the goalkeeper got down and made a great save, rescuing his team.

It had looked like we would really be up against it, but this was just about as good as the semifinal of the Africa Cup of Nations when we beat Ghana 3–0, when I think we probably played our best football. During the match, Dave Becker, our physiotherapist, turned to me and said, "This is one match I don't want to end." We were that good.

That night we delivered an excellent performance against a top team filled with world-class players. Afterwards, as we were walking across the field together, the German coach Berti Vogts admitted to me that this was the worst he had ever seen a German side turned inside out; he was very complimentary of exactly where we were going. I was delighted because hitting a high like this just before the Africa Cup of Nations was exactly where we wanted to be.

The encounter with the Germans proved that we were ready to go and I invited Jomo Sono to be a part of the setup. There had been an issue earlier when I had flown back to Durban and he had run a training session for me. When I returned the following day, I took over again and he didn't turn up for a couple of sessions. When I asked our team doctor, Victor Ramathesele, whether he had seen Jomo, he responded that Jomo was upset with me. Jomo thought I had undermined him by not letting him be more active in coaching. I said that he had never done any coaching for the national team, but told Victor to ask Jomo to come in and chat so we could clear the air.

Fortunately, common sense prevailed and everyone understood that things happen, that decisions affect people in different ways and that all is forgiven in the end. I certainly hold no grudges. So while Bafana enjoyed plenty of success and had many good times together, it wasn't always the case, but it taught us how to deal with adversity.

Playing in Africa was huge, and it came as something of a shock. When we arrived at our destination, we would find that the food wasn't always what we expected, so we ended up taking our own chefs. Unfortunately, you run the risk of being seen as trying to be better than your host and that leaves a bad taste in their mouths. It certainly made us a few enemies.

But by now, everything was in place and the country was looking at us to conquer Africa.

Trigo of Manning Rangers receives a celebratory and now customary kiss from Clive at the end of the match.

TEN

Motivation

"We knew we could win, because of him, because he believed it."
— ANDRÉ ARENDSE

There is no doubt in my mind that the night we played Ghana in the Africa Cup of Nations semifinal was a defining moment in South African football. We could have beaten any side in the world that night and Ghana had moved from a FIFA ranking in the 90s to a top-20 side just prior to the tournament.

That Bafana team was made to believe they could beat anyone and it showed in their success. I always emphasised that the players should never be scared of any other team, that they could play anywhere at any given time, and win. Rather than worrying about the opposition, I wanted them to focus more on what they could do, what their own strengths were and, if change was needed, then we'd change it. We had the capacity and the quality of player to do that.

It wasn't arrogance as much as instilling confidence. I always backed myself and backed the team – and that worked out more often than not for us. If the players take confidence out of their performances, then that self-belief grows.

My coaching philosophy has always been to make the players work hard technically to get themselves sound. The mental side of the sport – elements such as confidence and self-belief – is important, but the players also need to have the right physical preparation so that those motivational words actually take root.

I aim to make the coaching sessions interesting and enjoyable, and try to make the players happy and content, especially at an international level. I also got my teams very fit, very focused and very motivated, as well as making them take responsibility for their actions, which ensured that they made the right decisions nine times out of 10.

"Clive didn't think we were the best from a perspective of arrogance, but he believed we were the best and so we naturally started believing that," André Arendse affirms. "There is a fine line between being the best and being arrogant, but we always stuck to the line. That showed in our demeanour and in our performances."

My philosophy was always that you couldn't copy another team. You couldn't try to play like Holland or Brazil and then expect to beat them. After all, teams such as Holland or Brazil had years of experience, playing international matches on a regular basis while South Africa was condemned to sporting isolation. I knew that if my team could play to their potential, they could win, and I made my selections with that in mind.

I would never select a team around the opposition, but rather around how I wanted to play the game. Perhaps there was a little arrogance in that – which is good because that's what you need; all top teams have that – but I'd rather have the opposition adjust to our game than us have to adjust to theirs.

We were very sensible in consistently selecting the same team. Bafana were even called the Tried-and-Tested at one stage because there was a core of players who featured in match after match. The fans and people in the street were happy about that because they knew the team backwards, knew who would play and where. They could identify everyone in the team. In fact, if I were to walk the present-day Bafana team down the street alongside the 1996 side, everyone would recognise the 1996 players but not the current team.

"One of Clive's greatest strengths was keeping the core of the team together rather than handing out caps; this had the effect of making the team a family," says Emy Casaletti-Bwalya. "You could feel the togetherness they had and it was clearly an advantage on the field – the results speak of that. The players were decent, they were humble and that humility came from the top. It's so important how the top is run because it filters down to the players. How the coach treated people definitely set the tone and no one was bigger than the team. That came from the coach."

I believe that creating a family atmosphere and a warm environment in a team is the only way love, trust and understanding can be cultivated. When you put those commodities together when coaching and working with the players, together with consistency in selection (and although everyone has a bad game, it doesn't mean that's the end of the road for them), you have the seeds of success.

"Clive had the great ability to make everyone feel part of a winning team, regardless of whether you were on or off the field," Neil Tovey remarked. "That came from the love we had for one another, the sense of brotherhood or family that Clive instilled in every team he coached. That went for the guys on the bench just as much, making them comfortable and keeping them motivated even though they weren't playing. That is always a big issue for a coach: keeping those players intertwined in the team unit when they aren't playing. There were players on the bench who were captains of their clubs, big names in their local teams. But results ultimately reveal whether you made the right decisions and he got the results."

When Clive spoke to us in the changing room, we would be so full of energy and self-belief, as well as belief in the team, that by the time we were running out onto the field, every one of us thought he was the best player in the world, in the best team in the world, and that we could beat anyone on the day. I believe that's what you need at international level – self-belief – and it's exactly what he did for us.

Going into the Africa Cup of Nations, no one really expected us to go all the way, but after the first game, when we beat Cameroon 3–0 – remember, they were the top-ranked team in Africa at the time – Clive said to us in the change room afterwards that we could go on and win the whole competition.

His pre-game and half-time team talks were always inspirational and motivational. He might have sworn once or twice, but it was rare; he was a composed person and I can't recall many games where we were losing badly enough for him to shout and scream at us. The team's success mirrored his team talks. He might have a go at players, but he knew who he could do it to. He would scream at Mark Fish, but not necessarily scream at someone like Helman Mkhalele because he knew some players might go into their shells and not perform. He didn't rant or rave; he was calm and collected. If a player was at fault, he made them understand what they had done wrong, but always gave the player the benefit of the doubt to rectify their mistakes and perform.

– Doctor Khumalo (Bafana Bafana and Kaizer Chiefs midfielder)

George Dearnaley recalls much the same from his days at AmaZulu.

Clive knew how to motivate and manipulate situations. He understood different cultures. When you talk about motivation, there are different types and he would know with some players who had it harder than the white guys that he would have to take a different approach.

Joe Mlaba was Clive's favourite son in the team, but the naughtiest oke around. Clive was always saying things like: "You're the best I've ever seen," or "The opposition are scared of you," or "You're the best player in South Africa, no one else can do what you can do."

We'd be sitting there listening and we'd shake our heads and think to ourselves: But Joe was poor last week, what's Clive thinking? But then Joe would suddenly turn it on and he would be the best player in South Africa.

Or Clive would say to me, "You're absolutely useless, I don't know why you're in the team, you probably couldn't score a goal to save your life."

I would be dumbfounded and it would upset me so much that I would come out wanting to kill people in my quest to score a goal, just to prove him wrong. He knew that to get the best out of me, he had to wind me up.

In one game against Orlando Pirates he told me I was on the bench that day. At the time I was the top goal-scorer in South Africa and felt there was no good reason for benching me. I was livid, those are the games you want to play, and while I watched my team-mates, I was sitting as far away from Clive as possible to show him how unhappy and displeased I was with him.

We were losing 1-0 with about 20 minutes to go when he told me to go warm up. So I sprint up and down and he puts me on. I score within about five minutes and I run straight towards him to have a go, to say, "Look what I am able to do and you don't trust me to do it," and before I could get my chirp in, he says to me, "I knew you could do it!"

– George Dearnaley

Eric Tinkler has similar recollections of how I could get the best from him, also by goading him. "He seemed to enjoy provoking me, especially around my weight, as he knew that this would piss me off and make me work even harder. But we would always have a laugh about it leading up to the games."

André Arendse has very fond memories of playing for me, acknowledging how important it was for the players to feel valued. I knew that they would run through brick walls for a man who treated them like the professional athletes they were.

When people talk about Clive, they'll all say the same thing: he was a motivator, fun guy, father figure. But what has always stayed with me, working for and with him, has always been the fact that he is someone you would never give up for, even if you weren't playing for him at the time, but were part of what he was building.

There is a personal experience involving me and Clive, when, at a stage in my international career when Clive had stepped into the job of national coach, I had been called up to the national team between 1992 and 1995, but I just wasn't getting the opportunity to play. I was always the number two or three keeper – but then Clive came in. I was still number two to a few keepers and the thought went through my mind that perhaps this dream I held so dear and close to my heart was never going to happen and I should just give up on the whole idea of playing for my country. But on the other hand, I knew he was going to give me an opportunity, because he was that kind of person, who backed you.

Having that support from a coach, whether you were playing or not, stands out for me; being a part of what Clive had built.

In motivating players, he got the best out of us. Even if mistakes were being made or the game wasn't going well, there was always positive information. I think that stemmed from the fact that he trusted the ability of his players. Clive took a while to put together a squad that he knew, over a period of time, would succeed. Every single one of the players in the squad had different attributes and he was able to combine them all. You could see his ability to motivate players in different ways, because players had different strengths and each one knew that his particular strength was a link in the chain.

The motivation often enough wasn't football related. But the players understood what he wanted. In one incident at a team talk before a game against Germany, he singled out Doctor Khumalo as the focus and said to the players: "When you get the ball, give it to Doc." And to Doc, he said, "I don't want you to do anything with the ball, just stick it between the opponents' legs." Because he knew that was a strength of Doctor Khumalo's, and that he could get away with doing that. Players responded to that and after a game, win or lose, he would address the positives of each particular player and what he had done in the game. He always recognised that if it was your best, even if it wasn't good enough, that was okay with him. That took players to a state of being motivated for the next game.

But ultimately it all came down to what Clive had built. There is no denying that the team was a bit of a mess when we got to 1995. We came back into the international scene in 1992, we had a bad run, then Clive came in and stabilised things with his approach. He made believers out of players and that was the turning point.

– André Arendse, goalkeeper (Cape Town Spurs and Bafana Bafana)

Eric Tinkler also acknowledged the strengths that helped forge a winning culture.

Clive was, in my mind, a players' coach; players wanted to play for him because he gave them freedom to express themselves as individuals. His main strength was his player management skills; he could identify when a player needed to be uplifted and when he needed to pull a player aside and talk to them. He never tried to humiliate any player in front of the group and the players appreciated this.

Clive had an arrogance about himself as a coach and even though he is not the tallest man, he feared no one and no team and he instilled that belief into the players.

– Eric Tinkler, midfielder (Wits, Barnsley and Bafana Bafana)

"Clive's great strength was understanding and managing players; the mental side of the game, getting the best out of his players," says André Arendse. "Those were the components that Clive mastered."

Glyn Binkin, the Bafana team manager, sums up the motivational skills required.

He was an unbelievable motivator – that was one of his endearing strengths. He made every player believe that he was the best in the world. There were players in the team who were good, but he made them believe that they were super stars, to the extent that they were cutting photographs of themselves out of newspapers and putting them up on the walls of their rooms.

He understood the dynamics of the individuals within the team context.

There were many leaders and real characters in the squad. Mark Williams and Mark Fish were two, and Clive understood that you needed those characters. Since then, the administrators have probably tried to suppress the characters, whereas Clive understood the value of raising the profile of those kinds of players. Those characters were never bigger than the team, they knew what their jobs were and they would go out and do the business.

They would do it for Clive and they would do it for their team-mates.

– Glyn Binkin, team manager (Bafana Bafana 1995–1997)

Even though there was a fierce rivalry between Jomo Sono and Clive on the field, the two coaches always had the utmost respect for one another.

ELEVEN

Respect

"Clive created a brotherhood in which there was never any animosity."
— André Arendse

Respect is a word that commands emotion. It's not about fear or compliance, but rather about admiration, esteem and even reverence. The saying that *respect is earned* is central to the success of a sports team.

Should a coach disrespect a player, or even vice versa, there's a strong possibility that the relationship could break down irrevocably. Most coaches will accept that in young, excitable and impressionable sportsmen and -women there exists one potential fundamental flaw: that fame and fortune may get the better of them.

When that's the case, you risk running into all kinds of issues. I treated all the players with respect because of their innate skills and abilities, and understood that I couldn't keep too tight a leash on them or it would backfire on me and, in the end, it would be the team that would be the loser.

Respect goes both ways. I've always believed that the right team is the one you prepare well and work with for long enough that eventually it gets to a stage when you can allow the players to play off the cuff. All successful teams throughout the world are like that; coaches can only do so much to get the players ready and there comes a point when he eventually tells them that they're in charge once they're out there on the field, and if things don't go as planned, then it is up to the players to sort it out.

I thought the best thing to do was to get the players to play as they saw the game unfolding, to play with freedom – and they did that. Players hate being told exactly what to do and how to play; they don't want to be treated like robots.

An example, for me as an outsider, is a team like Manchester United under manager José Mourinho in late 2017. I would never tell Mourinho what to do, but if I could, I'd tell him to let the players loose a little and let them go out there and express themselves. Once you get a side expressing themselves, you have a sound team because they're doing the job they're meant to do.

I believe the players respected me as they did because I let them play off the cuff. I enjoyed it when they did and played well. When you beat a team like Kaizer Chiefs three times in a season, as AmaZulu did, then you know you're doing things right.

Emy Casaletti-Bwalya and I first encountered each other when she was with Kappa, sponsor of the South African national football team kit.

By 1996, Kappa had already been with Bafana for four years, the very first sponsors, but when Clive was appointed the new national coach, he was like a breath of fresh air. His demeanour was that of making you feel equal to him, unlike other coaches. And especially as a woman, where one had otherwise been made to feel a bit inferior, like you didn't know what you were talking about. Clive had that ability, which is quite a gift.

In those days, I was a woman, a white woman, in a male-dominated industry where it was very difficult to get respect until you showed that you really knew something about football. I appreciated the fact that Clive always treated me extremely well, not talking down to me but speaking to me as his equal.

Having previously dealt with Augusto Palacios and Stanley Tshabalala, what stands out with Clive is the way he treated me, he was always the perfect gentleman. He took your opinions and feelings into account, and that made us work even harder.

Also, he was not a freebie king, which was something very refreshing.

From a marketing point of view, we at Kappa found him to be a great ambassador, both for the game and for the country; particularly South Africa at that time. He transcended everything and cemented our thinking in terms of cutting across the barriers that existed in the country at the time.

One problem we had was when Clive wore our kit, we had to shorten the tracksuit pants for when he did his aeroplane run and he was a bit wider too, so we had to take extra-large pants and chop off the bottoms; he had extraordinarily short legs!

He commanded huge respect from the players, yet he maintained a playful relationship with them, which is a very difficult balance to strike, but he managed that.

– Emy Casaletti-Bwalya, Kappa representative

As an important and influential player, Doctor Khumalo understood exactly how this respect was earned and delivered.

Clive was like a father figure to everyone in the team. I think he knew that if you treat players like kids they'll behave like kids, but if you treat them like adults, which was what Clive did, they respond well. He'd allow us to make decisions outside of football, like if we were going to stay at the hotel or not.

Clive was good with the players and he understood that some players might need their own room or others may need an arm around them. Some might need time off and others might need time with family. He treated each player on his merits.

He was very much a man manager, rather than just a football coach. He fought for the players; he understood the value of making sure the players were the most important part of the equation, which included the fans, SAFA, the government. This was possibly to his own detriment. He would sometimes fight with the association on the players' or support staff's behalf and this would land him in trouble. He understood that by getting the players on his side, we would go out and do the business for him on the field. We loved him as we would a member of our family, and we were a family.

– Doctor Khumalo

André Arendse explains further that recognising the significance of respect and trust was a massive part of building the team.

Trust was a big word. We had just won the quarterfinals of the Africa Cup of Nations, the biggest event of our lives and we're going into a massive semifinal against Ghana, but the next day Clive came with tickets for every player, whether you lived locally or out of town, to go see our families for two days. This in the midst of the most important game we were going to play; because he had trust in his players. It was a two-way street, and every player, Mark Fish included, came back ready for that Ghana game.

The closeness that Clive built was an absolute bonus for the team. And whether you were playing or not playing, it was always about the greater good, Clive made every single player see that; it was just incredible.

– André Arendse

Lucas Radebe reflects on how the players reacted. There was never a master-and-servant relationship that might exist between a coach and his players where the coach is a god and his players there to do his bidding without question.

As a footballer, it isn't always fun playing internationally, especially when you return home from playing for your overseas club. But then you meet up with the other Bafana players. He made the team special thanks to his personality as a respectable coach. We were never his players; we were his brothers and sons. He wanted to help us achieve, that was his role and he played it perfectly, particularly with that 1996 team.

He was unbelievable; we had players who represented different clubs and he didn't worry about that, but he was a master motivator in the handling of players. He also treated us as adults. We'd had coaches who made sure there was security everywhere and were very strict about the movement of players in the camp. But Clive understood and respected who we were – a group of mature people who behaved professionally – and he treated us accordingly.

We appreciated that by respecting him back and it was absolutely amazing because everything just fell into place.

He gave us days off for haircuts or shopping or going to movies. No one ever thought about sneaking out of camp or missing training, because we were treated like professionals.

It wasn't only on the field where Clive showed his value, but even dealing with SAFA as far as money issues went, he was on our side. He supported us completely but he made sure that there was respect shown all round. This included letting us go out or giving us a night away to spend with our families at home. It worked very well for everyone and everyone made sure they were professional and responsible about it.

I wasn't going to even play in the AFCON tournament. He showed great respect to me by calling me and asking how I was and whether I would be able to play. I felt that I didn't need to only honour the national team, I also had to honour Clive because of the respect he had shown me.

He sent Dr Ramathesele to Leeds to assess me and to talk to the club to see if they would release me, especially as I was carrying an injury and they might be reluctant to let me go. Clive was a rare coach who showed belief in his players and would support them.

– Lucas Radebe, defender and captain (Kaizer Chiefs,
Leeds United and Bafana Bafana)

Despite pushing the limits and providing plenty of headaches to those who tried to keep him in check, Mark Fish understands the value of a coach who has the health, welfare and happiness of his players at heart.

> Clive understood the players individually; he knew how to handle Doctor Khumalo, how to handle the late John 'Shoes' Moshoeu, every one of us. The respect he gave us off the field was why we gave him so much respect on the field. And why we played the way we did.
>
> First and foremost, he treated players as humans, as the adults they are. I think all the players respected and highly regarded Clive as a coach and as a father figure. He led by example, from the front, and when I look back when there were debates about money and although Clive wasn't really involved in those discussions as a coach, if he had to be, he always supported the team.
>
> My first game for Bafana was against Mexico under Augusto Palacios who played me in about seven different positions in the space of 20 minutes. It was a big challenge for Clive when he took over; he adopted a team where I was fortunate because I was established in the team and everyone was talking about me. I was the central defender at Pirates but he wanted to make space for me and knew the way I played, so on the day of Nelson Mandela's inauguration, he still had Steve Komphela, who was getting a bit old, and he and Neil Tovey were the two central defenders.
>
> So Clive selected me in the middle of the midfield. He saw the game from a different point of view and would always make decisions to benefit the team and which, 99.9% of the time, did benefit the team.
>
> – Mark Fish, defender (Orlando Pirates and
> Bafana Bafana)

For André Arendse, the single most enduring and endearing memory is the compliment I paid him and his wife:

[Clive said] that if he had ever had a daughter, he'd want me to be her husband. That was a massive compliment coming from someone I have always looked up to and respected.

What he always did so well was take the time to have a conversation with someone who comes up to him in the street, just to say hi.

He's a true man of the people.

- André Arendse

When football engages with ballet. Clive and Yvonne tying the knot in Durban in 1967.

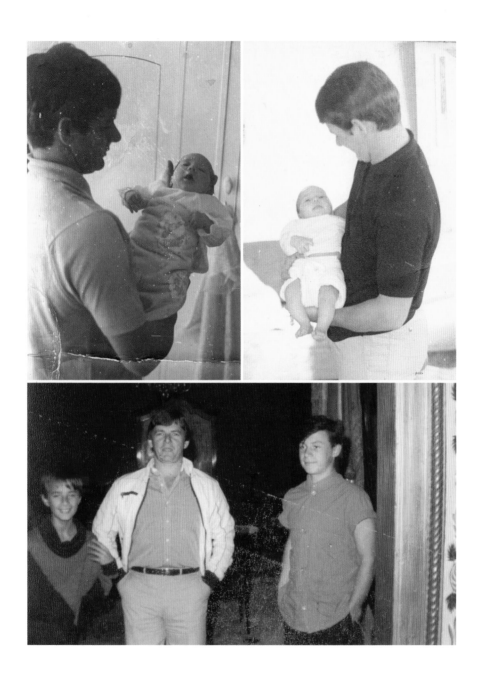

TOP: *Fatherhood. Clive takes care of his two sons. John (left) in 1968 and Gavin (right) in 1971.*

BOTTOM: *Growing Pains. Clive with his two boys on a trip to the Cape wine farms in 1980.*

TOP: *The Barker Boys. Clive poses with Gavin and John in Yellowwood Park in 1990.*

BOTTOM: *Durbanites. Neil and Clive have enjoyed a friendship on and off the field.*

Clive and Yvonne have been married for more than 50 years and shared many memories on that journey. TOP LEFT: *Purchasing a new house in Yellowwood Park.* TOP RIGHT: *Making breakfast for the family, not always a common practice over the years.* BOTTOM LEFT: *Enjoying dinner while on a trip in Greece.* BOTTOM RIGHT: *Cooking up a storm in Cape Town while Clive was coaching Santos.*

TOP: *Clive and Yvonne making a toast to John and Marilyn during their engagement.*

BOTTOM: *Bafana training session.* LEFT TO RIGHT: *Butch Webster, Clive, Mark Fish, Greg Wenster and David Becker.*

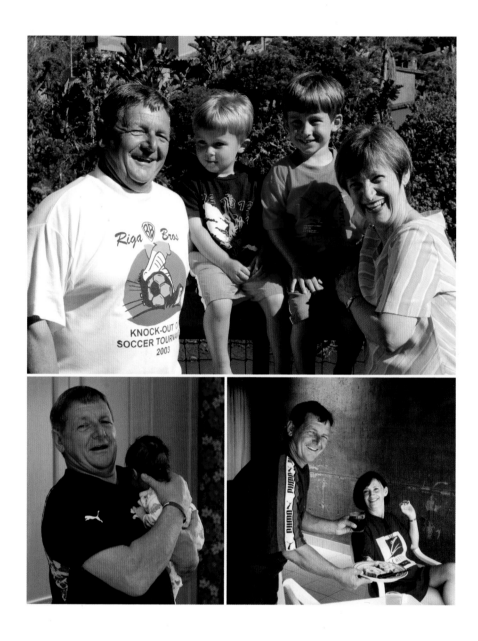

TOP: *Proud grandparents. Clive and Yvonne with Caleb and Garcia on the KwaZulu South Coast.*

BOTTOM LEFT: *New addition. Clive cradles Byron.*

BOTTOM RIGHT: *Lunch is served. Clive and Yvonne on a break in San Lameer.*

TOP: *Music Man. Clive gets the banjo out, entertaining Garcia, Caleb and Carl.*

BOTTOM LEFT: *Proud grandparents. Clive and Yvonne with their five grandchildren.* BACK LEFT TO RIGHT: *Caleb, Luca, Byron, Eli and Garcia.*

BOTTOM RIGHT: *Clive celebrates victory on the family bowls challenge. Luca and Eli not too concerned about the result.*

TOP: *The Barker Clan in December 2017. LEFT TO RIGHT: Garcia, Clive, Yvonne, Carl, Luca, Byron, Liza, Eli, Marilyn, Jon and Caleb.*

BOTTOM LEFT: *Taking care of the young ones. Clive with Caleb, Byron and Garcia.*

BOTTOM RIGHT: *The one that got away. Clive teaches Garcia how to fish.*

Clive holds the Webb Ellis Cup with former Springbok Morné du Plessis.

TWELVE

The Africa Cup of Nations

"Winning AFCON in 1996 was so much more than footballing success; it was a victory for social cohesion. For togetherness, for nation-building."
– EMY CASALETTI-BWALYA

n 1995, I drove up from Durban to Ellis Park in Johannesburg to watch the Rugby World Cup final between the giants of world rugby, the Springboks and All Blacks. In the car with me were my close friend Henry Naudé and Gary Halfpenny, a top-class footballer.

In a thrilling match in front of 63 000 people, the Springboks prevailed 15–12, having closed down the big threat posed by Jonah Lomu. Who could forget Joost van der Westhuizen's brave tackle, holding on for dear life as he stopped the gentle giant? The scenes before, during and after that epic match were unforgettable.

Afterwards, Springbok captain Francois Pienaar and Nelson Mandela made it a great day for South Africa, and the whole of the country rejoiced.

So did I, but I knew that the moment Joost passed the ball to Joel Stransky and the flyhalf drop-kicked the winning points, there would be huge pressure on Bafana the following year at the Africa

Cup of Nations.

Black South Africa wanted to be associated with a winning team and football was the South African sport with the greatest support.

After the Rugby World Cup Final in 1995 – and having consulted with the physio, David Becker – we decided to fly to Cape Town to find out how Morné du Plessis and Professor Tim Noakes had produced the goods for the Springboks. They sat us down and went through all the problems that might arise: sponsors' incentives, loss of form, deaths at home, injuries and all other scenarios we might be faced with.

I was very happy with our technical team of Phil Setshedi (assistant coach/manager), Dr Ramathesele, physio Dave Becker, event and team manager Glyn Binkin and kit manager Joseph Modisane. Jomo Sono was also there as chairman of the Technical Group.

We identified the fact that if we got through the qualifying group stages and top of the group, we could base the squad in one venue for the entire tournament. We chose the Sunnyside Park Hotel and stayed there for the duration, not having to pack and unpack after each game. The hotel staff was very accommodating, the chefs prepared our meals perfectly and the games room was also an important consideration.

We appointed legendary players to our technical team who acted as our scouts. Budgie Byrne, who played for England, scoring eight goals in 11 matches, delivered an astute analysis from Port Elizabeth; Mike Makaab, a debonair businessman and coach who could plan better than anyone I knew, provided insights into the opposition teams based in Durban; with Peter Nyama based in Bloemfontein. All three spent the pool stages checking out the teams we would possibly come up against in the knockouts.

They would send us the information, and without their help we would not have won the Africa Cup of Nations; they played a huge role.

Our preparations were going well because we had been able to put a programme together that saw us playing a number of top teams in the run-up to the tournament. The aim was to test the players against better and better opposition as we went along and that all culminated in us drawing with Germany (0–0) a month before. I don't believe there was much else we could have done to plan any better. Of course, there was always the weight of expectation on our shoulders, but we certainly weren't favourites.

"On one hand there was no pressure on us to win the Africa Cup of Nations because we were the minnows going into the tournament," explains team manager Glyn Binkin. "Yet, on the other hand, there was, given the success particularly around the Springboks in the Rugby World Cup the previous year. So in that sense, there was a lot of pressure, but that was where Clive was best because he took the pressure and expectation off us and put it on himself … We were a very united team; everyone would go and fight for us. It wasn't just the eleven players on the field – it was all the players in the whole squad. Everyone felt that they had a contribution to make and everyone contributed in their own way."

The build-up to the competition, having prepared ourselves against top international sides – culminating in the draw against Germany – set the tone for a successful Africa Cup of Nations tournament.

"The process of winning AFCON didn't start at the commencement of the tournament," says Neil Tovey. "We were, by that time, getting results and starting to be recognised. We qualified for the tournament and then got the nod that we would be hosting it. Beating Malawi 3–1 away from home – and other results that were starting to come to the fore – meant that the team started getting attention.

"There was an element of good planning; that element of high-quality opposition we were playing was all vital to our success."

But if the build-up to the competition was good, there was just one big doubt: the Lucas Radebe affair. Lucas had picked up a nasty knee injury and I worried that he might not be available for selection. Dr Ramathesele, who examined him, suggested we leave him out of the competition, because if we didn't, he'd break down. When I spoke to Lucas to deliver the bad news, he said to me, "Do yourself a favour and do the country a favour – give me an opportunity. I won't let you down."

Lucas was playing for Leeds at the time, for their second side, but he assured me he was ready to go and was feeling good about himself. I took a gamble and at the last minute included him. He was completely off in his first run, his timing out. Nevertheless, I made a calculated risk for his second game and played him in the back four. Although he managed to get through the game, we were beaten for the first time in a long time.

But from then on, I think he was the biggest factor in our success in winning the cup. He just got better and better as the tournament progressed. He was playing alongside Neil Tovey at the back and he looked really fantastic. He hit the right spots at just the right time and brought with him a special aura, and I believe that he was the reason we won the Africa Cup of Nations.

Lucas managed to get over all the hurdles and, going into the first game against Cameroon, I think the most important goal was getting a win. Like the Springboks the previous year with Nelson Mandela leading the charge, it was all go, go, go; we had to do the same. Cameroon were one of the favourites and to beat them would set the tone for the remainder of the tournament.

Everything was going right, although there was an issue when it came to light that Zane Moosa was unhappy about being left out. He had played really well in one of the warm-up games, but I had decided to leave him out. I called a meeting with him in my hotel room to clear the air and of course he wasn't very happy, but he decided to leave it all in the hands of Allah (and the coach) and, fortunately, he let bygones be bygones. I've always rated Zane very highly; I loved his style of play at Wits and he just got better and better at Sundowns and ended up part and parcel of the victorious Africa Cup of Nations side.

The conditions were perfect for that game. Although the ground was beautifully manicured, the grass was slightly longer than usual to accommodate the number of games the FNB Stadium would be hosting.

Shoes Moshoeu and Philemon Masinga were simply outstanding – they controlled the destiny of that Cameroon game. Shoes dictated, Philemon was quality up front, Eric Tinkler and Mark Fish were strong and resolute, with Doctor Khumalo good in patches. We were very fit, and the players seemed to have benefitted from the two-week break we had given them over Christmas. We were inventive, quick and efficient and never really looked threatened at any stage. In the end, we scored three goals against one of the top sides in Africa and ended up winning comfortably.

Cameroon were strong, but lacked organisation and looked a little flat – although they did improve as the tournament progressed.

So our opening game had all gone according to plan. Our finishing was accurate and defence was excellent. My final thought on this game was that we needed more performances like this. I was happy.

But there were detractors in the media. When I picked up the Sunday papers, the editor of *City Press* had written: "How can we trust this impudent schoolboy with a national treasure like the South African football side? How can he have sole responsibility over the fortunes of Bafana Bafana?"

And this was after we had won 3–0! Considering that type of press, I wondered what would have happened if we had actually lost. I believe – although I don't have the facts to back it up because he never said it to me – that he later made a public apology and admitted that he was out of order for saying what he did.

Our second match was against Angola. I retained the same team for what turned out to be our hardest game of the tournament. Angola were strong, quick, well organised and very skilful, playing with a lot of width, and we were fortunate to win. Although we were in great physical condition, I know that, on the mental side, we underestimated them.

The field was wet, heavy and very slippery from rain, making play difficult and, with the euphoria from the opening match still prevalent, I know determination was missing. The opposition also made life awkward for us by playing tight and making it difficult for ball-players like Doc and Shoes to express themselves.

But we came through in the end, with Mark Williams netting the only goal of the match, a rebound off the keeper. Philemon

Masinga had given another good all-round performance, Shoes Moshoeu was good in patches, while Linda Buthelezi had a much-improved performance from the Cameroon game. Eric Tinkler was magnificent, a true warrior, while Sizwe Motaung and Neil Tovey both put in sound performances. André Arendse had given his best performance to date.

I felt that a draw would have been a fairer reflection of the match, but that we needed to devise a system to offset the defensive attitude of the Angolans.

Our third game – just four days later – pitted us against Egypt, when things came a bit unstuck. The Egyptians played much like other North African countries: they were defensive, kept possession; were well organised and good at counter-attacking, they were also strong and technically sound, the influence perhaps of European coaches.

The only goal came from a free kick just outside our area. The shot was deflected through the wall and fell favourably for their captain Ahmed El-Kass to score. Although we lost 1–0, we had achieved our goal of heading up our group. We had six points going into the match, which offered us the chance to rest a few key players, but we still needed a convincing performance. I think, mentally, the players were not as sharp as they could have been, although we did actually play better than we had against Angola.

The Egypt game was our first defeat in 16 internationals, but we had made changes, compensating strength for flair, and paid the price.

I, however, had reservations about Augustine Makalakalane. When playing for South Africa at home, for some reason the public refused to accept him. This not only affected him but the team overall and I felt that the only way to consider him would be to select him for games away from home only. He had played a very limited role and wouldn't feature again in the competition.

Over the course of the pool stages, everyone seemed to gel and get closer and closer and we went into the quarterfinal against Algeria in good spirits. After the setback to Egypt, I had pushed the team hard at training; this was the knockout stage, after all, and there were no second chances. The players responded well. I knew the attitude had changed, that the motivation and determination were high and there was only ever going to be one result.

For the quarterfinal, we moved Lucas Radebe to the back, and Doctor Khumalo and Linda Buthelezi returned to the midfield. We identified that Neil Tovey was accommodating his lack of pace by backing off too much and consequently we were battling to get our midfield players to support our front men.

The first half against Algeria was the best we had played but all we had to show for it was a Doctor Khumalo missed penalty shortly before half-time. But then in the second half Mark Fish scored his first international goal for Bafana Bafana – only for Algeria to equalise with a header at the near post with six minutes remaining. From the restart, Shoes Moshoeu received the ball from Shaun Bartlett after Helman Mkhalele had made the running, played a one-two, and then another outside the 18-yard area was right in the box and side-footed the ball home. It was his second goal of the tournament, a marvellous goal – the most vital of the tournament – and we were into the semifinals.

This was a tough match because we never put it to sleep. We needed an extra goal but failed to score it. It was still a great team effort, though, much improved, and everyone contributed. We had delivered a confident, all-round performance. The change at the back had proved effective, as had the reintroduction of Doctor Khumalo, the midfield pairing of Eric Tinkler and Linda Buthelezi, and the flair and pace of Shoes Moshoeu.

Afterwards, the technical group discussed at length the problems we had identified, but ultimately we had to pay our respects to Peter Nyama for his insightful and accurate assessments of Algeria during the group stages.

We had won through to the semifinals where we met the Brazilians of African football, Ghana. Their star player was Anthony Yeboah, and Lucas told me he wanted the job of picking him up. I said to him, "You've got the job – just make sure you do it", and he was outstanding. Lucas's presence and his ability to defend was a big part of why we beat Ghana. Yeboah was marked out of the game.

But that night, it was the Shoes show; he really turned them inside out and we led 1–0 at half-time. Shaun Bartlett struck early in the second half when he got a through-ball and crunched it – he really smashed it, with extraordinary power and timing. This goal sealed the match.

Afterwards Ghana's Brazilian coach, Ismael Kurtz, walked up to me and handed me a Brazilian football shirt. He said he'd like me to have it because this had been the first time he'd seen a team play with the direction and discipline of the European footballers and the flair of the South Americans, all in one night.

This was the match everyone anticipated, the game of the competition, and the unofficial final. And they were right – Bafana delivered. They gave a performance that made major football personalities such as Michel Platini, Pele, Bobby Charlton and Berti Vogts sit up and take notice.

Although the 3–0 scoreline did not reflect our overall superiority, it was a night to savour. The atmosphere was electric and we were mentally strong; determination had been the key in a battle between two similarly skilful sides.

Every player was on top form. Among my individual performance assessments, André Arendse was "brilliant but safe", Mark Fish "outstanding yet again", Doctor Khumalo "brilliant", Eric Tinkler "strong and resolute" and Shoes Moshoeu, with his two goals, "a quality player". Lucas Radebe was the player of the night and Neil Tovey was outstanding – I only wished he was still in his mid-twenties.

Reflecting on the mix of precision and creativity that Bafana delivered against Ghana, Neil explains exactly how it all came together: "We had the depth and the blend – Clive knew what strengths he needed in his players and that Bafana team revolved around the capacity of each individual, playing as a collective. He wouldn't ask Doctor Khumalo to tackle like Eric Tinkler and he wouldn't ask Eric to dribble like Doctor. What each player brought was a component that was needed as a collective. We were probably so successful because we had that variety."

Glyn Binkin recalls:

The players did the business on the field, they were happy off the field, the fans were around, supportive of us and there was a great buzz and energy.

For me, it was like a blur; I had to pinch myself constantly to remind myself that this was reality, it was actually happening. And this blur wasn't just about the three weeks of the tournament, but a six-week period, including the build-up.

In the three weeks preceding the tournament, there had been a very good build-up to the tournament, some carefully planned preparation games and carefully planned preparation tournaments and come the competition itself, we were ready.

The opening game against Cameroon set the tone for the rest of the tournament. Even that loss in the tournament to Egypt was a wake-up call to perhaps take a step back. Perhaps if we had gone all the way to the finals without losing a game, we may not have won it. We had a sense of what losing was about and that became part of our preparation for the final.

– Glyn Binkin

But it wasn't all just football, and I understood that the players needed to get out, get away from the game and just be themselves. Now, however, there was a different component to this free time, because they were starting to gain hero status and people began to idolise them.

"Clive used to give us a lot of time off; if we played on a Wednesday, we'd have Thursday afternoon free and the guys would do their own thing in and around Sandton," Mark Fish explains.

"After the second game and once we had qualified, we'd walk around Sandton and people were recognising us. It was white people who knew who Doctor Khumalo was, or Shoes Moshoeu. Remember, this was in Sandton; we started seeing things and people differently, and they us. Particularly after the tournament, the public knew who Bafana Bafana were, whereas before they hadn't. We were famous!"

While many might argue that this was an incredibly talented team, I have said before that the Bush Bucks team of 1985 was the best I ever coached. But perhaps this was the *right* team at the *right* place and time.

"Many people might disagree with me that we probably never had the best team at that tournament, but I think we had the right team," André Arendse suggests. "In terms of player for player and mental strength, mixed with how much we wanted it, that all put together was the right mix. It showed in the results."

Eric Tinkler offers similar sentiments: "My memory of the team back in 1996 was that it was a very well-balanced team. It had great technically gifted players. It had speed, it had aggression and it had intelligence, but most importantly, it had a group of players who were hungry for success and with all the same common goal."

I really think that on that night of our semifinal clash with Ghana – and people might question this – we would have beaten any side in the world. There was a huge crowd and it all came together perfectly. This was a night when South Africa took all the frustrations at never being able to display our skills to the world out on Ghana. We were exciting, strong and brilliant – producing a night to remember.

It seemed like all the stars were in alignment and that took us to the final.

Clive encourages his AmaZulu players while conducting a training session on the beach – adding a fun element to his coaching techniques. (Anesh Debiky/BackpagePix)

THIRTEEN

Switch On, Switch Off

"It says a lot about Clive's coaching perspective that I don't believe one player didn't enjoy his coaching sessions."
– NEIL TOVEY

How do you determine a good coach? There is such a wide range of areas you could look at, but ultimately it always boils down to trophies – you're rated according to your success on the field. The Africa Cup of Nations was South Africa's greatest sporting success, but the pressure was overpowering. The important thing was to never allow the burden to get to the players; if they had too much on their mind, it could derail everything and, given how much was riding on our success, the players needed to have all outside, negative influences removed.

Playing in a tournament like the Africa Cup of Nations is daunting enough, but the weight of expectation on the team, as host nation, was immense. South Africa was a nation desperately in need of healing – and heroes to make that happen. So, to maintain focus on the job at hand, the players needed to be treated especially carefully. Making training light-hearted was one way of relieving some of the pressure.

I tried to make training interesting, to make it a little different, but also to be as practical as possible, especially when replicating the game scenario. I think there's nothing worse than getting down to training and all the coach does is send you round and round the field, making you run. There's a time for running, a time for playing and a time for everything else, and I think I generally got it right nine times out of 10 (not 10 out of 10, because you'll never get it right every time).

If, as a player, you're finding training a bind, you're not going to be eager or excited about it. But it's still a form of work that can't be avoided and I never believed in cutting training short; rather work them hard or they'll walk off the training pitch feeling cheated – and that's no good.

Eric Tinkler has fond memories of what it was like away from the pressures of the game, letting off steam, always making sure of the fun element.

"I can remember Clive surprising me with his singing qualities after the game against Ghana in the pub at Sunnyside Park Hotel. I had a friend of my father who could play a number of golden oldies on the piano that Clive would request and he did a fairly good job singing those songs, but I could not convince him to apply for Idols."

Lucas Radebe has the same recollections of fun. "One thing about Clive was that he got along with everybody; we used to have fun, we would joke, we would all laugh together. He was a real charmer, everyone fell in love with him, even to this day; he has such charisma. He's a one-of-a-kind coach."

My son Gavin recalls with a smile how I involved the family, but perhaps already had the decision made before asking for input from Yvonne, John or Gavin himself.

Our favourite restaurant was Giuseppe's on the Durban beachfront and whenever my dad had a major decision to make, that's where we would go for dinner and discuss the issue as a family.

My dad's footballing philosophy was always to take on the best; he was that good, with that good a team. And without disrespecting teams like Mauritius and Lesotho, he was interested in playing England in England or Argentina [who we drew with here at home].

One evening, sitting in Giuseppe's, we were discussing the latest proposed fixture – to play Germany without the Pirates players who were involved in the Champions League final – and we were trying to convince him not to. "Dad, they'll kill you; you'll be beaten 8-0. This is Germany," we argued. "You're asking too much of Bafana to play Germany and expect a decent result."

Although my dad would listen to us, he made up his own mind and I think our visits to Giuseppe's were rather just an excuse for us to have a family dinner together. He was always going to play Germany – he'd never have turned that opportunity down.

They drew 0-0 and Doctor Khumalo was brilliant, skinning the Germany captain, who was jerked, fuming, after that. Their coach said he'd never seen a team combine the flair of Brazilian football with the discipline of Europe like we did that day.

– Gavin Barker, Clive's youngest son

I think mixing it up sensibly allowed us to become successful. It allowed the players to reset, because if you put them under pressure, you're not going to get the best or anything extra out of them.

To be a good coach, yes, you need to have good players around you, so Clive was blessed on that level. But you also need to pick out the right combinations – you could have all the best players in the world, but if you don't blend them together into how you want to coach them, you'll never succeed.

Clive was very, very good at blending players. He knew where he wanted the backbone, or spine, of the team and then he'd build around that. His team concept was based around the exuberance of youth coupled with an experienced backbone.

What for me was a really good aspect was this: if you ask players, they'll tell you they don't enjoy training, they'd rather just play games. But what Clive did exceptionally well was to make training fun; we'd enjoy it. You can talk about match analysis and reading of the game, but I think it boils down to where you spend most of your time. The match is 90 minutes, but you train for hours all week and that association the whole week is where you see the coach and what he's about.

Whether you ask players from his Yellowwood Park days to Juventus, to Durban City, to Bush Bucks, to AmaZulu and finally to the national team and since, I don't think you'll find many players - if any - who will say they didn't enjoy Clive's training. I think that's where he ultimately found his niche. You used to enjoy going to training, and that's what it was all about. That's not to say we fooled around, it was focused - as it should be - but at the same time, it was always enjoyable because 90% of the time it revolved around scoring goals and that's what football is all about.

Unlike many coaches who emphasise all manner of training regimes centred around making the player better, faster, more accurate, Clive understands the basic principle about humans, and that's that people are human.

They need balance; all work and no play will upset the delicate equilibrium that high performers need to be able to perform at their best.

– Neil Tovey

André Arendse talks about trust levels – that a coach cannot give players flexibility if they cannot toe the line.

If players are given time off, they need to understand that they have a duty and commitment to their team-mates and their coach not to abuse that trust. Clive didn't ask for trust, he earned it and the players repaid him.

What Clive did so well was create a fun element along the journey. We'd finish a game and go back to the team hotel and we'd all end up in the bar having sing-alongs. He'd be having a beer with the players, he always wanted that to be done together, he never wanted anyone sneaking around, doing it behind his back. He wanted to be there with us because again, that comes down to the trust levels.

– André Arendse

Mark Fish, ever the fun guy, recalled the same sentiments during AFCON. "After every game, we would return to the Sunnyside Park Hotel and meet downstairs and everyone would have a beer, as a team, together. Some of us didn't know our limits, some of us did, and the next day we'd be training again."

This socialising didn't always go down well with those outside the team who might have thought the fun element was being taken to extremes. But I understood that the players needed an outlet to let off steam and by ensuring that it was done together, as a team, the family element would shine through along with mutual respect.

"We have to remember that players aren't monks; we can't stay in our hotel rooms – we have to live," Lucas Radebe points out. "Clive made things easier for us and he was very easy-going, which was what we needed at that time given the magnitude of the tournament."

After the loss to Egypt I thought the players looked a bit flat.

Although we were through to the next round, it was the first time that some doubt crept in. Perhaps there was a lack of confidence and on the way back to the hotel on the bus afterwards, I told everyone to meet me in the foyer when we arrived. We pushed back the piano, gathered round and sang a few numbers while Eric Tinkler's father's friend tickled the ivories.

With that, I saw the press sitting to the side watching in disbelief and could only imagine what headlines would appear in the newspapers the next day: COACH PARTIES AFTER LOSS.

Neil Tovey reflects back on this, and again the word *respect* comes out. It was definitely a two-way street.

When we beat Cameroon 3-0, the whole team went out afterwards, with the wives and girlfriends, and had a good time. This was during a tournament, completely unheard of in many teams; it just wouldn't be done. But that came about because of the respect we had for one another. The players respected Clive and he respected them; that they would know their capacities, their regeneration time and would honour their commitments to recovery and responsibility.

That was such an important area; the players knew they would come out the next day and if they had to train hard, they would. But we all went out collectively and that made us stronger as a team. That comes into the game, which you don't always see, but there are moments when things get tough and you need one another and that support comes out because you train together, you go out together, you do everything together.

Even during the preparation leading into the game, if guys wanted to go out and play golf or go shopping, they would have an afternoon off, which isn't something that is always considered by today's coaches. It's vitally important to strike the right balance between switching on and switching off and Clive knew exactly when he needed to do that.

It was a collective within the team and it might have been frowned upon in higher quarters, but while we were getting results, we could do that.

People think you have to train, train, train, but rest is just as important, and what kind of rest you have. You can sometimes bombard players with too much, you can see it, it does happen. So the balance between work and rest is so vital. I believe especially during tournaments, you prepare for five, six weeks before, then you play in the tournament itself, that could be three to six weeks depending on how far you progress. The cricketers have a nice balance where, at times, the wives come out, but they might be away on tour for three months. We can learn from one another.

This all comes back to the coach and the respect for each

other – if I have respect for the coach and he has respect for me, then there will only be one or two individuals that you need to keep an eye on, the prodigal sons. But you also don't want to stop the uniqueness of certain characters, like Mark Fish or Mark Williams. You need people like that who tend to turn dark moments into light-hearted ones. Clive allowed that; we used to take the piss out of each other all the time and you could either sulk about it or laugh along with everyone else and get on with it.

– Neil Tovey

Mark Fish admits that he must have been a real headache for me as the coach, but as Tovey suggested, you needed characters in your team, just as you needed X-factor players. It was always about striking the right balance.

We toured Australia and played our first game in Melbourne and the second in Sydney, and after that game, with a lot of alcohol involved, I was directing traffic at King's Cross.

Clive knew his team and understood us. And we performed for him. SAFA did right by appointing Clive as national coach; they saw something in him and Clive saw something in the players in his squad. For the Africa Cup of Nations, not only did we have a team he believed in, but the Federation also believed in the coach – there was no interference. And then there was the media who started believing what the Federation and coach were doing. Add to that the supportive fans in the stadium; Clive had this ability to pull everyone together.

I don't think he was given enough credit for that. You can pick a national team coach, but he must go out and do his job and Clive did it very successfully.

– Mark Fish

George Dearnaley spent a number of years playing under me at AmaZulu and loved his time there.

Clive was a great player's coach. The training sessions were always enjoyable and he was always enthusiastic and energetic. He was motivated and always excited to be on the football pitch and that translated to the players. We loved training. Training sessions define you and define your team because you spend much more time training than actually playing. There was always a good vibe, although there was also discipline; he would joke with the guys, motivate individual players, but you knew there was a line you couldn't cross. There were one or two guys who did cross the line and he pulled them right back in again. I think I speak for all those AmaZulu players when I say we all looked forward to going to training sessions. They were always fun, but organised, and there was always a great vibe and great team spirit in the camp.

Clive was a great motivator, but there was more to him than just that. He had been at AmaZulu longer than the players and he always made it seem so easy to integrate players from different backgrounds, races and communities. There was always humour, starting with him. He would take the piss out of players; it didn't matter who you were, if you set yourself up as a target, he'd make a joke about you, have a go at you, and that set the tone for the rest of the players. No one was immune – he chirped everybody.

Although we were only semi-professional back then, the atmosphere was always professional under Clive. We were there to work, to do a job, but you could do all of that and still have a laugh. We enjoyed each other's company. Clive also made himself the butt of the joke too; we'd refer to him as Mr B – some would call him Mr Boerewors (but only behind his back).

He loved getting involved during training, every now and then he'd want take a shot or put in a few crosses with his dodgy left foot and when he did something well, he'd tell us he could still play and that he still had it, that we could learn a lot from him.

– George Dearnaley

Ultimately, if the players need to be on top of their game, they also need to be allowed time to relax away from the game and I allowed that without them taking advantage.

Well, not too often.

*Clive shakes the hand of Madiba after being introduced by
Bafana Bafana captain Steve Komphela.
(Paul Velasco/BackpagePix)*

FOURTEEN

Madiba Magic

"Sport has the power to change the world."
— NELSON MANDELA

N elson Mandela had been freed and was an international icon. Next to religious leaders, no one could match his humility, love and understanding and he was embraced and accepted throughout the world.

Nelson Mandela was a true man of the people and I would regularly receive phone calls from him at home. One day the phone rang and Suzie de Villiers, my 10-year-old niece, answered. She then called me, saying, "Clive, there's a guy on the phone who wants to talk to you; he says his name is Nelson."

During the Africa Cup of Nations, we had the support of Nelson Mandela and I'd received a phone call asking if I minded if he came to visit. So it was that he came to the Sunnyside Park Hotel where we were based for the duration of the tournament. It was getting to a stage when he was getting a little frail and I asked Neil Tovey to take him around by the arm and introduce him to the players. I didn't trust myself with that honour because I was likely to pull him down with my own dodgy knee.

And, of course, his visits were frequent. There was such an

aura when he would arrive, he'd bring his grandchildren along and they would mingle with the players' children. I can remember him asking the families if they were too frightened of him to even say hello, such was the respect he commanded. They were so much in awe of him and of being in his presence that they just stood around, wide-eyed.

"Madiba had a lot of respect for people; whether you were young or old, he treated you with respect," Lucas Radebe remembers. "He also had great respect for Clive and whenever Madiba came to visit, like everyone else, he wanted to listen to what Clive had to say.

"I recall one morning when we had to wake up at 5am, which was unheard of and had never happened before, but we were going to meet Madiba and Clive was the first one there. In fact, I don't think he even slept that night."

Madiba had been a huge motivating factor in the Springbok defeat of the All Blacks when they won the Rugby World Cup the previous year, and a year later he exhorted Bafana Bafana to an even more meaningful victory.

Nelson Mandela was hugely instrumental in Bafana's quest to win. Whenever the team was down, be it after a loss or the vibe was wrong, we would always refer back to how he had gone through 27 years of imprisonment at Robben Island and what a leader we were blessed to have at that time; so what the hell were we bitching about?

He had spoken to us about the importance to South Africa of us winning; he spoke to me on the phone continuously throughout the tournament. He spoke to Clive all the time too. He was a very busy man and that gave the enduring thought that here was this international icon making time to speak to us, you couldn't do anything but run out onto the field and play out of your skin.

He was a unique man; in his presence you could not help but be inspired to lift yourself to great heights in whatever you were doing. To become better; not a better football player but a better person. When you become a better person you become better in all aspects of your life. That's where Madiba inspired us; he was very close to the team and understood the power to inspire that the Springboks achieved in their Rugby World Cup success shortly after the 1994 inauguration. He knew what sport would do for the benefit of the country and how it would unite the people as a nation.

Everybody loved him and everyone knew that when he was there, there was no way they could let him down. I wouldn't have been able to walk off the field after a game if we had failed him.

– Neil Tovey

When Nelson Mandela was released from a 27-year imprisonment on Robben Island, the world's most famous inmate became the most celebrated and influential figure in the world and he belonged to South Africa.

But the healing was never going to happen automatically. The fuel needed a spark and that had been provided by the 1995 Springboks when they won the country's first Rugby World Cup, defeating the mighty All Blacks at Ellis Park. But that spark needed something more to fuel it, to produce fireworks – and Bafana Bafana delivered in 1996. Where the Springboks might have attracted significant support from non-traditional fans, the black population, there was still some animosity around the composition of the team of 14 white players and one coloured player, Chester Williams.

If the country was to be transformed, sport needed to change too, and that meant building a multiracial support base, which the Springboks could not command in totality.

And then one sporting team did heed the call to action. Bafana Bafana embraced the notion of unity in deed and design; a multiracial, multicultural team who accepted the challenge laid down by Madiba who knew the power that sport had to unite.

Because South Africa needed unity.

In his iconic address at the first Laureus World Sports Awards held in Monaco in 2000, Nelson Mandela inspired the audience with a moving speech to honour international sportsmen and

-women, speaking volumes for the healing ability of sport in South Africa.

"Sport has the power to change the world," he said. "It has the power to inspire. It has the power to unite people in a way that little else does. It speaks to youth in a language they understand. Sport can create hope where once there was only despair. It is more powerful than government in breaking down racial barriers. It laughs in the face of all types of discrimination."

Mandela understood the power that sportsmen and -women had to inspire others to achieve greatness, on a level playing field where all are equal. Where fair play and sportsmanship are the rules that apply. Where a nation could unite as one people – South Africans – when their teams conquered the world.

There was no doubt about the influential Madiba Magic in 1995 and 1996. He not only inspired, he challenged greatness.

My eldest son John was witness to that powerful spirit too, realising what this gentle man could inspire.

I returned from England where I was living at the time to watch the tournament. Bafana kept winning, everyone was behind them and the country was gripped by an incredible spirit of excitement and inevitability. We'd won the Rugby World Cup the previous year and there was the great hope we'd win the Africa Cup of Nations in 1996.

On the eve of the final, my dad phoned me and said I had to come to the hotel – Nelson Mandela was arriving. It was so exciting and I drove with my friend Martin Beck and his girlfriend Samantha Jarratt Huxtable to the hotel. The three of us met up with all the players and the coaching staff – probably 35 people in total – in the hotel conference room.

Nelson Mandela arrived, and although he was accompanied by seven or eight very tough-looking security men, the tension in the room was more about the pressure on my dad and the players. Nelson Mandela sat down on a chair and greeted everybody and asked Clive to stand next to him. The two of them silhouetted together was a very special moment.

Nelson Mandela hugged my dad, who hugged him back, and then he spoke to the players, an inspiring team talk that, had they had to face Brazil, they would have beaten them 7-0. He told them: "It was important that the Springboks won in 1995, but tomorrow is more important for the country. You can't walk off the field as losers."

The poor players ... I could feel the pressure they were under. But what a magical half-hour in which he and my dad acted like old friends. It was beautiful. Afterwards, he signed everyone's shirts and when he got to Samantha, the only woman in the room, he said to her, in his most charming way, "You must be the striker."

Madiba would arrive at a stadium and turn the game around. We'd be 1-0 down to Zambia, [then] he'd visit at half-time and we'd go on to win. He was so involved in football and sport, it was amazing. He was the extra player that the opposition didn't have.

- John Barker, Clive's eldest son

Francois Pienaar alluded to the fact that the 1995 Springboks, too, felt like they were playing with 16 men.

"We had an advantage playing the Rugby World Cup in South Africa, with the Madiba Magic on our side. He was an unbelievable leader and we were very privileged to have him backing us. How he changed the mindset of South Africans in such a small space of time was infectious; I can only imagine the All Blacks when they saw how South Africans totally gushed over Madiba and chanted his name at the final – they must have sensed that we weren't going down without a huge fight."

Francois also hinted at the unity this amazing statesman brought with him.

"If it wasn't for Nelson Mandela, I don't think the entire country would have been behind us. This was the first time in our history when everyone was proud to support the Springboks."

Doctor Khumalo was another who was inspired and in awe at every meeting.

It was fantastic meeting Madiba; he encouraged us, telling us how important it was for us to go out and perform for the country.

Every time he came to the hotel, the experience I had with him was different. It's very difficult to describe because on each occasion there were different emotions. I was fortunate, along with Lucas Radebe, to have lunch with him and got to know him as an individual and what he stands for; and why he was such an important person to us.

Whenever he came, it lifted us as a team. He constantly instilled in us the importance of this being a game, but more so, what we could do for the nation. He reiterated this every time he met us. It boosted us and made us aware of what we were doing, the responsibility we had. It wasn't just 90 minutes of football - it was so much more.

The value of winning the Africa Cup of Nations wasn't about lifting the trophy but what it did for the country.

He motivated people beyond anything they could imagine.

– Doctor Khumalo

For André Arendse, reflecting back on the 1996 Africa Cup of Nations, it was clear that the country was coming together under Nelson Mandela's energy.

There were moments throughout the tournament that we felt the support of the nation, they embraced us. It still gives me goose bumps when I think back. Perhaps it was a time in South African history when everything was coming together. We were fairly new on the international scene - we were hosting Africa's biggest tournament; we had the entire nation supporting us, whether it was 93 000 people at FNB stadium or 45 million watching on TV. People would greet us in the street, saying "Hi!" or wanting a photo with us.

Then we had President Nelson Mandela visiting us every morning at our team hotel. He'd have breakfast with us and each time reiterate how important and valuable we were to the nation. We'd go out onto the pitch for each game, 1-0 up already, and the game hadn't even started yet!

A lot of people to this day will come up to me and say: "That '96 team was fantastic; it was the best team – that's why you won the tournament," but I disagree. It might have been part of our success, but there were many different components. We had the support of the nation … it was the Madiba factor. Even the way soccer was run at the time, it was for the players, which was one of the most important aspects of all because the players were happy. They wanted to put on the jersey because it was done with respect and a lot of pride.

You add all those components together and there is something special, but we could never have done it on our own – there's no way in the world. I believe that because of all those things, and then you throw in the home environment which counts for so much because the support is massive, it's difficult for a foreign team coming to deal with all that.

What stands out in my mind, and I can see it clearly now, all these years later, was lining up for the cup final against Tunisia and singing the national anthem in front of 93 000 fans. I could see black faces, white faces, Indian faces, coloured faces, all together. With all that united support, we knew we had to do it for them all. It was such a driving force and it worked; it absolutely worked.

I clearly remember not feeling any pressure, but I felt a massive feeling of support. We had the entire Springbok team from 1995 at the final, lining up on the side of the field with their trophy and that too was a motivating factor.

We valued the support we received and we knew we had to repay it. Because we had such different talents in that squad of players, we were able to pull it together nicely.

– André Arendse

Nelson Mandela truly provided the magic.

Clive is hoisted in the air in celebration by
Andrew Tucker, Roger De Sa and Daniel Mudau.
(Matthew Ashton/PA Images)

FIFTEEN

The Final

*"You'd think that by now, more than 20 years later, there would
be new heroes, but I don't think anyone has really usurped
those players from 1996."*
– Clive Barker

I woke up on the morning of the final, probably one of the most
monumental days of my life, with a stark awareness of the
magnitude of what was expected of us. The range of emotions
running through all of us added to the hype of the occasion. We
were excited, nervous, happy and optimistic. But there was pressure,
plenty of it. The burden of expectation was enormous and although
it was wonderful having Madiba around, that only added to the
weight we were already carrying on our shoulders.

Everyone was switched on that day. He had been at the
Sunnyside Hotel with us, together with the wives and girlfriends of
the players and the squad. That morning at breakfast, I was joined
by the Minister of Sport, Steve Tshwete, who took a call from a
rather worried Minister of Police who reported that there was a
crowd at the stadium pushing down the walls and barriers, trying
to get inside.

Black South Africans had supported the Springboks in the

previous year's successful Rugby World Cup and, in a show of support and reconciliation, many white fans booked their tickets online for the football final. However, black fans who had been supporting the team from the very start of the campaign found themselves unable to get tickets through the usual channels. So when they arrived at the stadium but couldn't get in, the Minister gave the order to open the gates to allow them in. If the capacity was 60 000, there were 80 000 people there, some hanging from the rafters.

It was the most incredible feeling, but it could also have been a disaster. By making the call, Minister of Police Steve Tshwete had taken a chance, risking injury to a lot of people. He was a tough man, a top-class person and I loved him. After the celebrations following our victory, he really got into the spirit and at one stage put his arm around me and said, "Clive, take me to the toilet or I'll fall over."

Finals are special. I like the quiet and solitude of going into a Cup Final dressing room early and I was pleased to get the opportunity for this final too. I love the calmness before a match; I could fall asleep there.

On that day, everyone was nervous and uptight and, of course, in a match like that, you have to play it down or emotions and nerves can get the better of some players. If you're playing a team at the bottom of the league, you as the coach have to talk for a long time, but if you're playing against the top sides in the world, you don't have to say much; your side is motivated as it is.

We were the only team in the competition that never warmed up on the pitch; we would do it in the car park every time we played. We were happy to do it there and the players decided that this was how we would do it each time. It was a chance to be a little bit different and perhaps avoid the excitement and public scrutiny in a quiet place.

Like all finals, it's really about the team you select and how you play on the day, and I remember that I had to make a decision to play either Shaun Bartlett or Mark Williams. Mark had played in nearly all the games and scored regularly and there was no reason to leave him out beyond a gut feeling and a decision based on tactics. I felt that Shaun was quicker, although Mark will deny that and argue the point.

They would have been equally good choices; I just went with Shaun. And when I announced the team, I looked across at Mark who I had left out and he showed no emotion – I thought he would, but, to his credit, he wasn't bigger than the team or the occasion. He was a big man and he took it the right way. When we left for the stadium, he was the first to lead the singing on the bus; he really seemed to have taken it well.

He could have been sour about the decision, but he came on to play a huge role. So, despite what must have been hugely disappointing for him, he got his reward after all. With 20 minutes to go in the game, I made a double change and brought Mark on.

There were times when I had to make those kinds of decisions, but in the end, I think they balanced out well. In saying that, in football they say only the guys who start actually like you and the others will tolerate you at best, hate you at worst.

Mark was still involved in the game, though, having been selected on the bench and I later heard that he was poking his head around whispering, "Tell the coach to make a change." He had readied himself to run on, shin pads in place, but as he sprinted onto the field, he shouted and his false teeth shot out of his mouth. I looked at the players, they looked at me – no one was going to pick them up for him.

The history books record that Mark scored both goals in the final. The first, in the seventy-third minute when he headed home a chip from Eric Tinkler, with the clincher coming a couple of minutes later when Doctor had the ball, looked up, caressed it down the channel and Mark ran onto it and put it away, probably saying to himself, "The first goal was for the country, but the second was for you, Coach."

In the team talk before the game, I told the players that because of the way Tunisia were coached, we needed to remain calm, to not allow them to go forward and certainly not give them a goal because if they got ahead of us, they would be difficult to break down.

This was never going to be an easy game. The Tunisians were very organised – not very adventurous, mind you, but accurate in dead ball situations.

The whistle blew to start the game and, early on, Mark Fish got himself deep in Tunisia's half and then played a one-two outside the box before smashing the ball at the Tunisian goal, hitting the crossbar. I shouted at him that I had told them to be calm and he replied, "Don't panic! Take it easy, coach!" Clearly, he wasn't going to heed my advice to just soak up the pressure.

We did manage to play with a lot of restraint, though, and before half-time I sensed that the pressure was getting to Tunisia and the altitude was starting to take its toll. Despite their speed upfront, they lacked variation and ideas.

Bafana Bafana, on the other hand, were mentally strong and had peaked at the right time. The weather conditions were perfect for this historic occasion, pitting the Eagles of the North against the Pretenders to the Throne.

It was a good, concentrated performance. We never panicked; rather, we were like Baby Jake 'Slow Poison' Matlala.

Afterwards, we identified a number of important factors that influenced our victory. Playing at the FNB Stadium was one, as was the altitude. The input of the technical team – Jomo Sono, Mike Makaab, Budgie Byrne and Peter Nyama – was astute and their observations of the strengths and weaknesses of the opposition proved invaluable. The Sunnyside Hotel provided the perfect home base, while we also enjoyed wonderful support from our sponsors, SA Breweries and Kappa.

Not to be discounted was the quality time the players enjoyed at home with their families. The regular and timely visits by President Nelson Mandela bound everything together with electric energy.

SAFA President Stix Morewa gave the team wonderful support and there is a saying that rings true here: *If it's not right at the top, it cannot be right at the bottom.*

We had scored lots of goals in the build-up – three in the first, one in the second, two in the fourth, three in the fifth and two in the sixth – and had shown that we certainly had the ability to score. Over the course of the tournament, we had played six matches, won five, scored 11 goals and conceded just two.

Afterwards, I showered and then stayed in the changeroom until there was no one else but me. I like that part of the game, especially when it comes to cup finals, which come and go in a blur. The hype is there, the noise from the crowd is deafening, the emotional roller coaster of the game itself, the prize-giving, it's all so intense and often you don't get the opportunity to actually soak up the experience and create the memories.

There was tension that morning … The pressure was on us and had you asked us at the start of the competition how far we thought we'd go, I would never have suggested that we'd go on and reach the final, but here we were sitting, against dangerous opposition but not opposition we were fearful of. We had respect for them but we could not let ourselves down after where we had come from. We had the likes of Cameroon, Angola and Egypt in our group.

It was a day we just had to make complete. And we needed concentration for the entire game, not just a few minutes; it would require a peak performance from us, which I think the majority of the players carried out on the day. It wasn't the most elegant performance of the tournament, but it was professional. We didn't give too much away; I don't recall us giving them too many opportunities throughout the course of the match.

The pre-match talk revolved around Clive inspiring individuals, inspiring the collective and not trying to change too much. You don't want to change your routine just because you're playing in a final and Clive never changed his routine. He is as superstitious as cricketers wearing the same underpants for match after match. He had his routine and never deviated from it.

– Doctor Khumalo

There is no doubt that there was huge value derived from the country's football success, following on from the previous year's Springbok triumph in the global rugby showpiece.

"The Rugby World Cup was about the whites in our country with some integration from the other races, but with the Africa Cup of Nations, it was exactly the opposite," Neil Tovey explains. "It was probably 98% of the nation behind us, with the remaining 2% completely unaware that this tournament was even happening. The Springboks definitely kicked it off and they gave us immense inspiration, but the effect was small compared to what Bafana achieved; we were touching everyone's lives."

When it came to the presentation, I received my medal and then walked up to Nelson Mandela and handed it to him. I put it around his neck and addressed FW de Klerk and King Goodwill Zwelithini and said to them that I couldn't give them one each; I was giving mine to Nelson Mandela.

When I think about what Mandela did for us as a football team, and what he did for our country and for Africa, I was delighted I could do that. It was a small thing, but he was such an inspiration to us and I'm sure the Springboks who won the Rugby World Cup the previous year will testify to that too.

The sacrifices he made – being on Robben Island for so long – and what always amazed me was that he never had a bitter word to say about anyone. That's why I gave him my medal. I thought then and still do that he's the greatest statesman this country (and the world) ever produced.

It all just seemed to fall into place. It was a beautiful, sunny day, the fans were literally hanging from the rafters and it appeared to be our destiny to win, to honour Nelson Mandela, and we certainly played for him that day. And once the tournament was over, there were the parades through the streets of South Africa. It was a magnificent time for a united country.

I remember going to Cape Town a couple of days later and as I walked past a group of ladies, they asked if I was the Bafana Bafana coach. I said yes and they said they were thrilled that, as a Christian,

I kept looking up to the sky during the final. In truth, I was looking up at the clock, watching it tick down. They thought I was saying a new prayer each time I looked up.

So, as much as that victory brought me and others so much joy, it was tough too – the nicest time, yes, but certainly the hardest of my life. And, with that said, we can also not ever take away from the contribution that the AFCON winning side of 1996 did for the country. To this day, if that side had to walk down the road in any big city, everyone would gravitate towards them. They were heroes.

I think that their popularity also had a lot to do with the fact that there had been much consistency around the side that had been picked – even people who didn't know football got to know the players. I think, overall, that is the biggest reason, still today, why that side was so revered. There's a reason why that team was loyal to the country, and why the country has been so loyal to the team.

In fact, those of us involved in the 1996 AFCON would like it to be won again. Because there's nothing worse than, every time you give a talk, people asking the same question: Why has South Africa not won any major tournament since 1996?

Zambian legend Kalusha Bwalya, with the benefit of 12 Africa Cup of Nations tournaments, six as a player, sums up the situation nicely.

Although the Africa Cup of Nations victory was 22 years ago, 1996 remains everyone's reference point to the tournament. That's how much winning the tournament means to South Africa. You came out of the apartheid era officially in 1994 with the first democratic elections and became African champions two years later.

It was an opportunity for South Africa to open itself to the world and we knew how important it was with Madiba's presence. Seeing the rainbow nation, people black and white on the streets and at the stadia, it was a momentous occasion. It was one of the best Africa Cup of Nations tournaments for me; I went to six as a player and a further six as an official and it still stands out for me. Many AFCON tournaments have passed since then, but it remains fresh in my mind still to this day; many people remember it because of its significance ...

We took 50 years of independence to achieve what South Africa did in two. You had good players, good management, good coaching and the Madiba factor.

Although there was an array of big stars in all the teams and it wasn't an easy period to win the tournament, there was no other way it was going to go down.

– Kalusha Bwalya (Zambian International)

Lucas Radebe fondly recalls the way the team banded together, a happy unit destined for success.

When I think back to 1996, mostly, I recall the atmosphere around the training sessions, around the training camp. It was really great; we felt that we had a chance. We were so positive, with so much belief in ourselves. We'd have a night off and Clive would tell us to bring our wives and girlfriends to dinner together, which was very brave of him. But that made it so enjoyable.

Even now, I can close my eyes and see Clive coming out of his hotel room, smiling, laughing, encouraging us. But when it was time to be serious, he was and we knew it.

The pressure on us was there, we knew that. We were hosting the tournament in South Africa and because it was at home, expectations were high. But we had an experienced team with great names and Clive made sure the players were successful because names alone don't win you games. He made sure we performed. He orchestrated our success, he was instrumental in that.

– Lucas Radebe

For Mark Fish, the unity of that day transcended all else and brought him particular happiness and contentment. The 1995 Rugby World Cup-winning Springbok squad arrived at the final as a show of support for their brothers in football and, like the fans in the stadium and South Africans glued to television sets and at shebeens, pubs and braais, cheered Bafana Bafana on to glory in our millions.

"What the Springboks did, coming to support us and visiting us in the changing room is the way sport should be: united and uniting," says Mark. "Probably the most memorable recollection I have of the Africa Cup of Nations was walking around after the final, wearing only my underpants. I'd thrown my boots and entire kit into the stands. One lady even wanted my underpants, but I'm sorry to say, I still had to preserve some dignity."

*Flying Man ... Clive performs his flying man celebration. It was his
signature and upset the touring Brazilians.*

SIXTEEN

The Flying Man

"Amazingly, 18 years later I was in Brazil for the 2014 World Cup and when I told the concierge at my hotel I was South African, he immediately did the flying man celebration."
– GAVIN BARKER

Having won the Nations Cup, the profile of the country rose exponentially in the greater football world. Our potential when we returned to the international fold in 1992 had finally been realised and Bafana Bafana, the new kid on the block, was being embraced across the globe.

It was a great PR story: the birthing of a potential football giant from a country previously marginalised by the international FIFA body. The sports embargoes of the 1960s, '70s and '80s had played their role in transforming South Africa from an apartheid state to a new democracy. And that democracy was now showing its might on the sports field – rugby world champions and, more importantly for our ANC-led government, a successful football team.

The nickname Bafana Bafana had caught on and spread like wildfire among local and African reporters. The *Sowetan* newspaper had bestowed the nickname on the team, but it had lost its flavour as we struggled in the first two years of our return to international football. Our successful run in the Nations Cup had reignited it and every fan and foe now referred to the team as Bafana Bafana.

The name made the news, however, when our opponents for the Nelson Mandela Challenge were announced. The international headlines read – BAFANA BAFANA TO FACE WORLD CHAMPS. It took some effort from the PR companies promoting the match to explain to the international media that what they were hailing was a match between South Africa and Brazil to take place at FNB Stadium in April of '96.

Every football kid's dream, including mine, was to represent his country against the might of Brazil – the country that brought samba to world football and dominated it, winning the World Cup three times in 1958, '62 and '70. Legendary names such as Pele, Garrincha, Zico and Socrates were spoken about in awe.

As I grew older and became a coach, that dream did not leave me – to test my abilities against the best. I had to pinch myself to remind me that it was now a reality.

To stir up fan support for the match, I stated that the best way for us to honour Madiba was to go out and beat Brazil – to show that our win in the Nations Cup was no fluke. The media had a field day, claiming that my ego had got to my head. They were right: we were playing Brazil, reigning world champions, who had won their fourth title two years earlier in America.

By all accounts, Brazil were bringing a strong squad made up of the stars that won the title in 1994, plus the best of the youth team preparing for the Olympic Games. Their two top players at the time – Bebeto and Rivaldo – had insisted on being included because it would afford them the opportunity to play a match honouring Nelson Mandela. The team also boasted the likes of Cafu, Dunga and Roberto in its ranks.

I admit that I thrive on a challenge to prove doubters wrong and, in the lead-up to the match, I worked the players into a frenzy, instilling in them the belief that they could beat anyone – including Brazil. I convinced myself and the team that we were world-beaters and for the first half of that match we were. Footage of the first 45 minutes of that match shows how we made a great Brazilian team look very average and why I think Doctor Khumalo is the greatest player I ever worked with.

It's hard to put a description to Doc's performance that night; all I can say is that he purred like a cat, dictating the game from the start, passing and dribbling his way into the heart of the Brazilian defence at will. The Brazilians did not know what hit them and, after intense pressure, Doc's floating corner was headed home by Phil Masinga and the stadium erupted. Then Doc turned from provider to goal-scorer with a brilliant goal: a volley from the edge of the box.

It was surreal, but as the half-time whistle blew I looked up at the scoreboard and it read South Africa 2 Brazil 0. I looked at the Brazilian players as they trudged off the pitch and they were shell-shocked; their legs were heavy and they carried the very real prospect of defeat in their eyes. Someone told me later that it was the first time in their history that Brazil were losing 2–0 at half-time in an international friendly; I like to think that was true.

When the second goal hit the back of the net, I had charged onto the field with my flying man celebration, arching my run in front of the Brazilian bench, something that incensed their coach, Mário Zagallo. As we left the field for the changing rooms, he gave me a look that could kill.

For the first time in my life I did not know what to say to my players. I thought of trying to bring them down to earth, but I could not get the smile off my face. My mind was filled with images of grandeur: if this team could make Brazil look average, could we build a team capable of qualifying for the World Cup, competing with the best, going further in the competition than any other African team had before, and even win it?

In that moment, all seemed possible, but then Doc delivered the killer blow: he was buggered and didn't think he would be able to finish the game. He suggested he be substituted.

I was angry and, out of character in my dealing with him, I had a go at him, telling him to suck it up because we needed him. My ego was getting the better of me – I did not listen to someone I should have.

Doc had run himself to the point of exhaustion in the first half and he was being honest with me, trying to warn me that he was going to be a liability. Against teams like Brazil, attack is sometimes the best form of defence and we were about to lose our attacking kingpin.

I should have made the change at half-time, but imagined the response of that expectant crowd if we had emerged after the break without Doctor in the line-up. I thought that another 20 minutes with him on the field and we could be 3–0 up and the game would be over as a contest.

But the half-time break robbed Doc of his energy and, no longer able to dictate the game from the midfield, the Brazilians took control. They had been stunned in the first period and what had started as a routine friendly match became something more. They were being humiliated by this unknown Bafana Bafana team.

"At half-time the Brazilian photographers that were covering the game were upset, lambasting the likes of Bebeto and Rivaldo for putting up such a poor performance in a match that honoured Nelson Mandela, embarrassing the great Brazilian name and tradition, but at the same time praising Doc and Clive," recalls my son Gavin, who was covering his first full international as a photographer. "I was so proud to be hearing that first hand. I was on a high, but the one guy cautioned me that Brazil would bounce back in the second half – that the coach would be hammering them in the changing room, threatening them that their careers, no matter who they were, would be finished if the second-half performance followed the first."

What Zagallo said to them at half-time I will never know but it had an immediate impact as the laid-back performances that we had witnessed from Rivaldo and company were replaced by real ability. They began to play as if the World Cup trophy was up for grabs and we were up against what I had always feared: a Brazilian team with a point to prove.

Flavio pulled back one and the manner in which they celebrated indicated they were in no mood to lose the game.

I tried to defend our position, but as soon as that goal went in, they had the game under control and there was no way through defence or attack that we could contain them. I took Doctor off – to the dismay of our fans – and boos rang around the ground.

I could not believe what I was hearing … Three months earlier I was the darling of those very same fans and now they were criticising my judgement even though we were still 2–1 up against Brazil.

But there had been a shift in momentum and the writing was on the wall. The great Rivaldo levelled matters, celebrating in front of our bench, and four minutes from the end, Bebeto completed the comeback, scoring one of the best goals I ever had the misfortune of being on the receiving end of – a scissor-kick, connecting with a high cross that sailed into the top corner. As I lifted my heavy head, I saw Zagallo and the rest of his technical team running in front our bench performing my flying man celebration.

Amazingly, we were booed off that night … How fickle support can be. "You are only as good as your last match" was the warning ringing in my ears as I made the long trek up the FNB tunnel.

If I thought the fans were bad, the press really got stuck into me. The headlines the next day read:

Barker's tactics deny Bafana famous victory.
Barker sacrifices attack for defence – tactic backfires as Brazil Samba to victory.
Does Barker have the tactical ability to lead Bafana to the World Cup after his naivety in replacing Khumalo turns victory into defeat?

It was only years later that I realised the impact that first half had on the Brazilians. I was in Brazil and when I explained to a few locals who I was, they immediately started doing the flying man celebration.

"I got the chance in Brazil during the 2014 World Cup to ask a senior journalist why the Brazilians still remember that match and that moment of celebration so well," says my son Gavin.

"He answered: 'We're Brazilian. We follow each game, even if it is a friendly, as if it is a cup final. They [South Africa] were laughing at us, laughing at Zagallo, one of our legends. You never disrespect our football – we take it that serious. But we also like characters. We love the passion that football brings out in people even if it is the opposition – their coach had passion – he was a character.'"

The silver lining of that miserable defeat was that the Nations Cup honeymoon was over and the reality of preparing a team for the World Cup qualifiers had sunk in.

Clive and Lucas Radebe share a joke during a training session.

SEVENTEEN

The Personalities

"[Mark Fish] was an orang-utan, but he never caused any ugliness."
– CLIVE BARKER

During my coaching career I have had the incredibly good fortune and immense honour to work with some of the most talented footballers this country has ever seen, as well as with other football personalities.

Norman Elliott, the Durban City chairman who played such a significant role in my early coaching career, was one of the greatest marketers in South African football. He really knew how to promote the game. Although he had made a name for himself in the hot-rod game and on the horse-racing scene, this snappy dresser and flamboyant personality was regularly to be found on the front page of the newspapers.

Could he usurp Abdul Bhamjee as the greatest impresario on the South African footballing scene? Also a great character and smart dresser, Abdul ran a huge sporting business in Fordsburg. He wasn't, however, always on the right side of the law and ended up serving time, although he was released early on good behaviour.

I visited Abdul in prison on the eve of the Africa Cup of Nations and, as I walked down the passageway, the inmates were shaking the bars and chanting *Bafana, Bafana, Bafana*. It was just like in the movies: the noise built up to a crescendo and I knew I would have to deliver. Nothing else would be good enough.

It was these two who had wanted their own versions of a BP Top 8 final: Norman wanting Durban City to play Kaizer Chiefs, but losing so that he would get the match fee but not have to pay out bonuses, while Abdul had envisaged a very lucrative home and away final featuring Chiefs and Moroka Swallows.

There can be no denying their immense but colourful contribution to South African football. Today Abdul lives in Johannesburg, but is no longer involved in the sport. How the game misses him.

The third memorable character was Afzal Khan. A genius as a football manager, Khan's knowledge of every player in South Africa was encyclopaedic. He won the league with Manning Rangers, Santos and Sundowns and should have been involved with Bafana Bafana but for a missed opportunity to invite him into the national setup. Had he been involved, I would have allowed him the luxury of keeping an eye on our overseas-based players, while his ability to work with foreign coaches at the highest level would have helped with the club-versus-country obstacle, which is an ongoing issue in many sports where players would rather represent their overseas clubs for the money than their country out of a sense of patriotism.

The national team lost the opportunity to include this top-class manager for a second time when he wasn't given the chance by his good friend Gordon Igesund.

When I was chasing down the League-Cup double with Santos while Afzal was there, Santos had been on the receiving end of numerous dubious decisions and I suggested to Afzal that should it happen again, we should stage a walk-off mid-game.

We were playing Moroka Swallows at the Rand Stadium and I caught up with the referee as he was walking down the tunnel to get the game started and pointed out a few of the decisions that had turned games against us. He promised to be partial and assured me he would ref the game as he saw it.

True to form, the ref awarded Swallows a penalty and I

challenged the decision – to no avail. At half-time, I waited for him in the tunnel and told him that Santos would not be coming out to play the second half and he could award the game to Swallows.

I confirmed my decisions with Afzal and he agreed to stand by me. I also briefed the Santos players of what had transpired and should the referee enter the changing room, they were to look like they were packing up to go home.

After the regulation period of the half-time break had elapsed, the referee came into our changing room and, to his horror, realised that we were indeed packing up halfway through the match. He challenged our decision to abandon the game, just as we challenged his decision to award the penalty against us, a dubious one at best.

I then addressed the Santos players and told them to produce the best second-half performance that they were capable of, warning our usual penalty-kicker to be prepared to take a spot kick. Moments after the second half kicked off, the referee blew a penalty kick in our favour, equalising matters. We scored to make it 1–1, although a good game was spoilt when Swallows scored again to win the game 2–1.

While a coach always has his favourite personalities, emotion should never get in the way of doing the job, which for me was to coach the best Bafana Bafana side I could assemble, and when the time came, to do the right thing.

Neil Tovey and I had travelled a long journey together and had become very close, as any successful coach-and-captain combination should. But all good things must come to an end eventually. Sadly, they're often the toughest episodes of your life.

> I personally don't think Clive's biggest achievement was winning the Africa Cup of Nations, but how he dealt with the captaincy issue. When we played Zaire in Togo, Clive had a big decision to make. Neil Tovey, his captain who had lifted the trophy, wasn't good enough to be in the team any more.

He needed to make space for another player to take over and to find a new captain. [Clive] had someone in mind, and he called three or four of the senior players and told us what he was going to do. We told him he had our support.

This was a World Cup qualifier and he made the decision of not only dropping the captain of the team from leading the team, he wasn't playing – he wasn't even in the squad. He would be watching the game from the stands. It was a massive decision that had to be made and nothing against Neil, all players need to eventually move on and that was an integral part of the process of us going on to qualify for the World Cup.

Sentiment cannot come into the equation; as a coach you need to make the right decisions for the team. I think that was Clive's gift: that no matter where we were in the world, he made the right decisions for the team.

– Mark Fish

Of course, it was easier on the heart when you identified a player to be included in the team; it was a positive for everyone.

I had watched André Arendse develop as a goalkeeper under the guidance of Mitch d'Avray for Cape Town Spurs. André was fit, skilful and brave, with the athleticism and grace of a ballet dancer. He had wonderful hands and reflexes and, importantly, possessed an exceedingly bright footballing brain.

Steve Crowley was the incumbent and number-one choice for Bafana Bafana at a time when, to help with our development as an international football side, we would participate in competitions featuring the best teams in Africa.

During the Four Nations Tournament, sponsored by Simba Chips, Steve was having an indifferent period as a goalkeeper when things kept going wrong and, during the match against Zambia, I substituted him. We held on to draw 2–2, but there were times when we looked no more than ordinary.

This was the match, however, that heralded the beginning of André Arendse's international career. He was such a consistent performer that when the Bafana team was named for each match, he and right back Sizwe Motaung were near-automatic selections.

Then, of course, there was Mark Fish – the lovable rogue. Mark tested my patience – and my sanity – but he was a true character and contributed enormously to the Bafana Bafana team, not only on the field.

Early in my tenure as national coach, we embarked on a two-match series of friendlies against Australia. On the Sunday night after the second game (we lost both, 1–0), I was walking in King's Cross, which was a really rough area, and I saw a familiar figure standing on the central island, directing traffic. It was Mark Fish. I knew he could only get into trouble and dragged him to safety.

Mark was an orang-utan, but he never caused any ugliness. He was the guy who always stretched the limits, but he knew when to back off, when he was pushing the boundaries too far. He was wise enough to know that.

He was a super player and fantastic person; I really loved him.

The first time I met Mark he was in hospital, recovering from a car accident, all trussed up. It was clear from the beginning that something was always going to happen around him.

Mark certainly did a few things wrong, but that is what his personality is all about. He was great for the team, even if he tested the boundaries at times. In fact, he didn't just overstep the mark, but leaped through the door, never hiding his immense presence.

Mark Fish does not deny it.

"When we played Holland in the Nelson Mandela Cup and Clive selected a B team, because on the Saturday was the World Cup qualifier against Zambia, I was one of three players who decided that we would go out and have some fun, not forgetting there was the qualifying match coming up. When I woke the next morning, I wasn't in the hotel room, like I should have been," he recounts.

"I called Glyn Binkin, the team manager at the time, and asked him to tell Clive that I'd go to the gym, I would do anything as penance for missing the training session, and he told me to just make sure I got back to the hotel. As I did, the team bus arrived back from practice and I stood there sheepishly, my tail between my legs, knowing I had really messed up this time."

It had taken me 40 minutes to realise Mark wasn't even at the training session. It must have felt like a dagger to the heart for him to find that out. As the players left the bus and walked past him, they were all laughing and I instructed him to meet me in my room. The look on his face showed that he thought he was in real trouble, and that I'd probably send him home.

"I had no excuse ... I was ready to accept any punishment that Clive would deal out," says Mark. "So I went up to his room, knocked and entered. He told me to sit down, looked me in the eye and asked me if I had a good time. I said yes, and he replied, 'Make sure you don't do it again.' And that was it. He knew how to handle each individual and each situation."

Mark Fish was a larger-than-life character who always seemed to be in the thick of the excitement. When our physio Dave Becker suggested we bring some Wits physio students in to do some of their training with us and give us massages after the first game of the AFCON, I thought it a great idea. Mark was single at the time so, in retrospect, it probably wasn't such an inspired suggestion to let him loose on these lovely ladies.

Mark got his massage and the next thing the young physio arrives, draped on his arm, at an SA Breweries function during the tournament.

"Things happen – as they do – and within the space of a week, she's in love with me," Mark recounts.

After winning the final we landed up at the Randburg Waterfront, everyone in high spirits – both emotionally and of the alcoholic kind – and while we were all celebrating winning the Africa Cup of Nations, I ended up consoling Mark's partner, knowing that this wasn't going to be the love affair of the century.

> I would have to say, although he would pull his hair out dealing with me, he knew that my intentions were always good. He'd tell me that we were playing an important game that day, and to please stay at the back because I was a defender. But the first time I'd get the ball, I'd go to the front.
>
> He allowed me to play my game and I think that was the

case with each individual in the team. He respected each player's strengths. Linda Buthelezi might not have been the most skilful player, but he was hard as nails and he'd get the team going with his tackles; the same with Eric Tinkler. Then you had the flair of Shoes and Doctor, who could create something special. He allowed each individual to express their God-given talent and that's what made the team so successful.

I'm sure I gave Clive more grey hairs than any other person he's known.

When I think back to the quarterfinal against Algeria, I'm sure I took a few years off his life as well as adding a few more grey hairs. Before the game, Clive pulled me to the side and said, "This is a very important game – please, just defend for the first four or five minutes; just defend and do your job." I said I would, but knew, deep down that it wasn't going to happen and the first time I got the ball, literally within the first two minutes of the game, I was in the opposition 18-yard area.

I remember looking back at the bench, watching Clive pulling at his hair in frustration. But he knew; that was just me and he allowed me to be me.

– Mark Fish

Despite playing at the top level of football, there were always going to be disappointments for players and tough choices for me. But their reaction to being dropped, for instance, showed what great people they were and how much they understood that the team was bigger than the individual.

"A lot of those players are still involved in football, which is a good thing," says Mark Fish. "I'm genuinely pleased that so many stayed in the game. I have no doubt that the Africa Cup of Nations success and Clive's interaction with them played a key role in keeping them involved in the sport."

Clive discusses tactics with former national team coach Trott Moloto.

EIGHTEEN

Troubled Times

*"We had a love-hate relationship, but that's common between
coaches and the media."*
– CARL PETERS

While it is easy to reflect on the good times, the successes
and the celebrations, coaching can be tough and the
players don't always behave. Then there are pressures,
expectations, personalities and instructions, both from inside and
out. As coach, there's a delicate balancing act to play.

There is also a fine line between keeping players in check and
giving them the freedom to express themselves as sometimes hot-
headed, sometimes just plain mischievous and mostly just being
young men among their team-mates.

But it wasn't always fun. There were many occasions in my
coaching career when, either by design or bad luck, there was a lot
of trouble to fix. Sometimes you use your smart mouth, other times
you leg it away from the action.

One year when I was coaching Durban City, we had played a
game in Joburg and got the result. We boarded the plane to fly back
home but, as everyone knows, the on-flight service only happens
once you're airborne and while the plane sat on the runway waiting

to take off, the players asked the air hostess if she could serve the famous brew early. She explained that this wasn't possible but that she would make a concerted effort to serve them first once we were in the air.

As she moved upfront, the players moved quickly and grabbed the beers, wine and some cold drinks. Eventually we took off and our willing hostess started to serve the players, as promised. Halfway down the aisle, she ran out of beverages and summoned the bursar, who checked for himself and then had to make a most unwelcome call to the rest of the passengers, apologising that the bar was closed and only tea or coffee would be served.

When we disembarked, I noticed that quite a few bags looked rather full but thought nothing of it at the time. Then during our Tuesday training session, Norman's sports car flew into the parking lot and he stormed out, ordering Butch to cancel the session and to get all the players into the players' lounge.

Norman had a habit of pointing his finger in a peculiar way when things weren't going right and he did it this time, spluttering that SAA had contacted him and were investigating what had happened to the alcohol on a certain flight. He produced an invoice for R800, which back then was a tidy sum of money.

To the players' credit, they admitted to taking the alcohol and the full amount was settled the following day. But we were told in no uncertain terms that this would never have happened before and that we had tarnished the club's name and image, and had inconvenienced the other passengers.

Guilty as charged.

I think we all ended up singing 'Shanty Town', 'Bye-Bye, Blackbird' and Vera Lynn's 'We'll Meet Again'.

Kaizer Motaung was a very elegant footballer, mature, with extraordinary balance. He played upfront and was able to score a lot of goals. He brought the famous gold and black colours back from America where he played and excelled. I have the highest regard for him and, as a player and later administrator, he had no peer.

Kaizer made huge sacrifices and I wonder how much pressure he was under, politically. But he called the right shots and built a very successful football team, as well as a name for himself and his family. He always put his family first and I can't say enough good things about him, as a player and an administrator. Kaizer Chiefs' record speaks for itself, and of course I have personal links, having played them so many times in cup finals – even though we were beaten nearly every time.

He was more than able to run and administer the best side in Africa, but lost out on playing opportunities, given our status as a political pariah and the associated sporting isolation at the time.

When we eventually became a democracy, we turned away from dark times. The country was a fireball; everyone wanted change.

The IFP supported AmaZulu while ANC members were for Pirates or Chiefs or, for that matter, anyone from Joburg. At one stage, AmaZulu were playing Sundowns, who were top of the league; we were in second place, and we never touched the ball that match. They hammered us and with that, having lost the game, the IFP supporters turned on the ANC supporters and all hell broke loose.

While cars were being smashed – Sizwe Motaung's BMW was petrol bombed – we were rushed into the changing rooms for our own safety. The fighting continued outside, but it was getting later and later and we were still stuck inside. Eventually we decided to make a run for it. We had the bus brought closer and climbed aboard. The players pressed their bags up against the windows for protection – and not for the first time either; we had had to do it years before. With that, George Dearnaley, turned around and said, "Hey, coach, but in those days they had sticks and stones, now they're armed with AK47s."

Albert des Neves, our director, had been sitting next to me, but following George's words was now cowering under the seat in abject terror, mouthing, "We're going to die, we're going to die."

The driver put his foot down and we were able to escape.

In 1994 we took Bafana to Australia to play two friendly matches. We had only just started playing international football and, after beating Zimbabwe and Zambia in our first two games, wanted to test the team a little, especially as we had the 1996 Africa Cup of Nations qualifiers coming up.

For the second match on tour, we had been booked into a hotel that boasted its own nightclub and, after dinner on the Wednesday evening, we all went our own separate ways, either back to the team room or to our hotel rooms.

But one or two guys wanted to check out the nightclub. Then there were three or four of them, apparently there for just one beer. A few minutes later, there were five or six. I walked in and the look of horror on the players' faces almost made me laugh – if it wasn't such a serious issue, of course. They knew that they'd been caught out and when I asked what they were doing there, they replied that they were just checking it out. "Just one or two beers, guys, then you must go," I told them in my strictest voice. We were here to play – and hopefully win – a football match, not party it up.

But as I stood there, more players arrived, until there were seven, eight, nine, ten of them. "I'm a little bit disappointed in you guys," I said. "But you are a team and you're standing together. However, there is one true professional among the team, and I know he's in his room relaxing and focusing on the game. And that's Steve Crowley."

Two seconds later, who walks in but Steve Crowley!

Headaches weren't only reserved for misbehaving players, but also player selection, as in the Lucas Radebe vs Philemon Masinga conundrum I found myself faced with when I was asked my advice as to which player was the better option when both were at Leeds United.

Both Radebe and Masinga were starting to shine at club and international level and their agent from Durban, Johnny Brooks, sent them overseas for an opportunity to play at Leeds United.

Leeds, unfortunately, had a very conservative supporter base, but with the promise of some English Premiership action, both players tackled their respective tasks.

From time to time, I would phone Leeds manager Howard Wilkinson to obtain the release of Lucas and Philemon to play in the various cup competitions in Africa and although he wasn't the easiest person to engage with, he would eventually relent and release them. He was fair enough, but the selection of both players for Bafana became a problem as the team became stronger and more successful around the Africa Cup of Nations and then qualifying for the World Cup in France in 1998. I would hear the frustration in his voice each time I called him to release his players to the South African cause.

One day, the phone rang in my office and on the other end was Howard. The first thought – or fear, actually – was that he was calling to tell me Lucas had popped a knee. Fortunately, it was no such catastrophe; he had phoned to ask for my advice on who he should choose between Lucas and Philemon as he only had room for one of them in his squad.

Although they played in different positions, Lucas a defender and Philemon a striker, this decision had the potential to have a huge influence on their careers. So, after careful deliberation – but what a tough call to have to make – I suggested he choose Lucas, which turned out to be the right choice because he went on to play with distinction and honour for Leeds. He is still revered there.

Howard Wilkinson later went on to manage the English national football team, while Philemon Masinga moved on to play in the Italian league where he scored many great goals against top clubs.

But it was an awkward decision for me to make. Both were legends of the game, good friends and great players. It was indeed a difficult choice; I hope I got it right.

Although I'm not a gambling man, coaching always presents headaches where taking a gamble may be the only solution to a serious problem. While spending the Christmas holidays with family down the KwaZulu-Natal South Coast in 2012, I received a call to coach Brian Joffe's Bidwest Wits team, which needed help. I left San Lameer and travelled back to Durban to meet Brian at the Hilton Hotel, where he asked if I would be interested in joining his club. Wits were struggling and placed eleventh on the log and, since I had never coached in Joburg before, I decided to accept the challenge.

When I arrived for my first training session, I joined up with a super technical team that included André Arendse as goalkeeper coach. The team and staff gelled together nicely and we had a marvellous run, finishing the league in fourth place.

"I had officially retired at the age of 42, having been very lucky to enjoy longevity in my career, and took up a goalkeeping coaching job at Bidvest Wits," André Arendse recounts. "The club was between coaches midway through the season and the CEO asked for my advice on who we should get to coach us and see out the season at the very least. There was only one name and I told him that he had to go fetch Clive, which he did and we started building a team."

I asked him to be my assistant, during which time we had a complement of four goalkeepers in the squad. Within about two months, disaster struck when, in the space of a few days, we lost all of our goalkeepers to major season-ending injuries. One had a fractured knee, another suffered ankle ligament injuries that required surgery and my last goalkeeper went down with a badly broken leg in the ninetieth minute of a game against Orlando Pirates. I sent on the 16-year-old I had on the bench and he conceded the only goal of the match, in the ninety-second minute. What devastation!

It was too late to sign a replacement, so we had an important decision to make: did we use a 16-year-old or a 45-year-old who was an experienced goalkeeper, but now retired and acting behind the scenes as a member of the technical staff? Would André Arendse be good enough, and what if he picked up a major injury? He had been inactive for about three years already. We called André in and discussed the pros and cons with him and his wonderful wife.

We still had a few more games to go before the end of the season and when I asked André what we were going to do, after some thought, he suggested that the final decision lay in my hands and that he'd go with whatever I decided. So I told him: "Fine, you're playing." At that stage he was 45 and he still suggested that I consider his choice carefully.

"I played the very next game and absolutely hated it because all of a sudden you don't see things the same way; the body takes a pounding because you haven't played at that level for three years," says André. "It was very difficult."

We selected André to play Tuks in his return to club football and I knew that my nephew, Steve Barker, and Sammy Troughton would send their gangly Senegalese striker, Mame Niang, to throw everything he could at André.

The first opportunity came by way of an early cross. André moved towards the flight of the ball but misjudged it completely and missed it by a mile. Such was the difference between match practice and the real thing.

But fortune certainly favours the brave and once André's feet began to move, his timing improved and we got over the line. Just being out there was tough enough so we were grateful for both the win and the three points.

"I played and throughout the game I kept thinking to myself, for goodness' sake do not concede one through the legs," André remembers. "We won the game 2–1 and luckily the goal against me was scored in the top corner and as it went in I was thrilled – I'd take that because any goalkeeper would have battled to save that shot."

We went into the next game with André again in goals and, with an inspiring display, everything fell into place. We picked up another three points. Thanks to André, we were getting closer to the top of the league.

Again came the choice: should I gamble and keep playing André, or should I call it a day? We had qualified for the Top 8, mission accomplished.

But what would have happened had André done a knee or ankle?

I pulled him aside and told him I had been forced to play him, but the family backed my earlier decision and wanted him to continue to do so.

So it was that I picked him for his final match and then said, "Enough is enough," and did not include him again.

What a team man, what a player. Maximum points.

"That experience, for me, was my career coming full circle," said André. "All those years I'd spent working for Clive as a player, to now be working with him on a coaching level was absolutely inspirational."

Although most of my life has been spent around players and all the fun and games they managed to get up to, sometimes with an absolutely crazy outcome, I had my share of detractors who didn't make things any easier. While I was trying to put out fires, others were throwing petrol onto open flames.

Every coach in every sport has one thing in common: dealing with the press. When you're winning, they hang on to your every word. But string a few losses together and it's a different story.

When we were in Saudi Arabia, Carl Peters from the *Daily News* was the one to break the story that the directors of SAFA wanted to get rid of me and he came and told me that. I asked him how he knew but he wouldn't say where he had got the information. And the mood between us was turning rather unpleasant.

When I joined Manning Rangers in 2001, Carl was on my back again, suggesting it was time for me to move on. But we got a result that night and, although I'm a terrible loser, I am an equally terrible winner too. As he made his way towards our dressing room, I slammed the door in his face and told him, less than politely, to leave. He opened the door and told me I had no right to do that – and promptly slammed the door in my face. From that day on, whenever he had the opportunity to stick the boot in, he did.

As Bafana Bafana coach, Clive and I interacted regularly as I was covering football for the *Daily News* at the time.

Clive invited a number of media to the national team's hotel on the eve of the final and through that I got to meet Nelson Mandela, who was also there to wish the team well. It was very social in a way only Clive could make it; he's a good human being.

There was never a cold, business-like relationship with him as coach and us as media.

In 1997, I was at the Confederations Cup in Saudi Arabia covering Bafana. The night before, I alerted him to the fact that the administrators wanted to let him go, which surprised him. He was taken aback when I phoned him in his hotel and told him the news.

Later on, our paths crossed when he coached at various clubs. This included Manning Rangers where Clive found himself in a bad situation. Part of my job at the *Daily News* was to analyse results and performances of the KZN teams and at one stage the stats didn't look at all good for the club; they had lost something like six of their last eight games.

After one game, I went to the changing room to get some comments from him, and he swore at me and slammed the door on me, telling me to get out and refusing to talk to me. He accused me of having incited the fans against him.

His reaction came as a surprise to me, because I had just done my job. The situation had become clear that he wasn't going to last; not through his own fault. Later, Manning Rangers were relegated and ran into major financial hardship. Along with that were unity issues between the directors.

Many years later, he was about to get released by AmaZulu and with the *Daily News* enjoying a good relationship with the local clubs, we got to break a lot of stories before the other newspapers. We had received word that AmaZulu were going to release him and after the story appeared in the papers, Clive contacted me to say that the painting contractor at his home had asked him if he was sure he'd have money to finish the job, because he had read in the paper that Clive was about to be fired. Clive wasn't aware.

We had a love-hate relationship, but that's common between coaches and the media, and of all the coaches I've dealt with over the years, Clive is probably the most human of them all. He was always very approachable and relaxed – save for those one or two times. There's no taking away the record of greatness attached to his name.

– Carl Peters, reporter

Clive celebrates with Bafana Bafana midfield star John 'Shoes' Moshoeu.

NINETEEN

The Road to the World Cup

"Unsettling things were starting to creep in."
– CLIVE BARKER

There was no easy route to the World Cup, no automatic qualification; we did it ourselves.

It was a tough ask and we had to play the better teams in Africa, but fortunately we won all our games except one – away from home against the Congo. That match in Brazzaville was the most frightening episode in my footballing career.

Playing conditions in the rest of Africa can sometimes be absolutely, shockingly ugly. When we played the Republic of Congo in our first-round World Cup qualifier in April 1997, we arrived at the field – the same venue at which we were to play our match – to train and found that the army had surrounded the ground. FIFA regulations allowed teams the use of the same facility for training purposes as for the game, but the army was having none of that – they had their own ideas.

As we made our way towards the field, one of the soldiers cocked his rifle and put it to my head. Mark Gleeson assured me he'd sort it out and I retorted, "That's easier for you than me – he doesn't have the gun pointing at your head!" But, fortunately, Irvin Khoza lived up to his nickname of the Iron Duke when he walked straight up to the soldier and grabbed his rifle from him.

It was a drama-filled experience. Our press and TV guys were all chased away from the match and we weren't allowed in the dressing rooms. We should really have just gone straight back to the airport and flown home.

And the match itself proved just as tough. They really got stuck into Mark Fish, who walked off at the end of play absolutely battered and bruised. It was hard going and we well and truly lost, but with everything that had happened, I don't think any of the players were focused enough to be effective. We were pretty dominant and lost just two games out of 29 in Africa and that was one of them. The other was during the Africa Cup of Nations against Egypt, but fortunately the losses didn't derail our campaign.

We had beaten Malawi home and away in our first two World Cup qualifiers, but then had four or five months before we would play Zaire in our next match and a Four Nations Tournament was held in the intervening period.

We wanted to handpick our opponents for this tournament just so that we could test ourselves, selecting who we believed were the top two sides in Africa, those playing the most attractive and successful football – Kenya and Ghana – as well as Australia.

It was a successful tournament for us, and we remained undefeated against all three sides to maintain our continuity and momentum for the upcoming qualifiers. We beat Kenya 1–0, Australia 2–0, and in the final game drew 0–0 with Ghana.

Then it was back to business. We went on to beat Malawi twice, as well as Zaire both home and away and inflict a comfortable 3–0 defeat over Zambia at home. We were just about there, but a 2–0 loss to the Congo away from home just after the Four Nations Cup meant that we still had a job to do in our final qualifier in the return leg clash at home.

The build-up to the World Cup culminated in the last game, against Congo, where we needed one point to qualify. We were just about home and dry and had really done well, but Philemon Masinga was going through a hard time because of a loss of form and he decided that he wanted to make himself unavailable, because every time he got the ball, the crowd boo-ed him. He was never going to look like Shoes Moshoeu, Doctor Khumalo or John Moeti, but I still tried to talk him out of it and into playing. I told him to worry about his own game and, if he did, he could turn around all the negativity aimed at him.

It's been shown again and again that when Doctor Khumalo picks the ball up in the middle of the park and pushes it through the defence, the ball comes over the shoulder of Philemon Masinga and he hits it in the screws, beating the goalkeeper as the ball dips over the goalkeeper's outstretched hand and screams into the back of the net.

Masinga then did what we all wanted him to do – he ran towards the supporters and turned his back to them, pointing at his jersey and shouting: "Spell my name! Spell my name!"

That goal took us to France.

Having qualified for the 1998 World Cup Finals, I sat down and presented a plan to SAFA in which Bafana would play the top 10 teams in the world, or at least as close to the top 10 as possible. I felt that after qualifying for the World Cup we needed to play the best opposition possible.

We were scheduled to play England at Old Trafford because the historic Wembley Stadium was being rebuilt, and the opportunity to play at this famous ground, steeped in footballing tradition, was a tantalising prospect.

I assembled a team and we flew out of OR Tambo International Airport on a Saturday night before booking into a lovely hotel in London on the Sunday morning. I looked forward to spending a week with the players.

We were set to train at Maccersfield not far from our hotel, but after breakfast there was a loud knock on my door. I opened it, only to be confronted by captain Neil Tovey and his right-hand man, Lucas Radebe. We sat down and then they dropped the bombshell: they were going to strike because their bonuses had not been paid and their slogan was 'No Money, No Play'.

I tried to negotiate with all the skill of a Houdini magical act, urging them to be sensible about what they were embarking on and about what they were doing to football in general, but they were adamant and dug their heels in – they were not going to give in.

So it was that I asked for an audience with the SAFA hierarchy and cancelled Monday's training. I then informed the president, Molefi Oliphant, of the problem and the potential embarrassment. What made matters worse for me was seeing the likes of Helman Mkhalele, John Moeti, Mark Fish, Mark Williams and Neil Tovey zipping around on carts every time I looked out onto the golf course.

It was the same on Tuesday and Wednesday. On Thursday, Irvin Khoza – the Iron Duke – arrived and at midnight I was invited to a meeting with him and Molefi. They were very accommodating and asked me where I stood on the matter. I answered that if the players went home, I would accompany them. I did not want to lose their trust and support and knew I had to make this decision in their favour.

Mark Fish believes that the players stood firm as a team: "I think we were getting paid about R10 000 each, but we had heard that the Federation was being paid £500 000 for the game. So we asked for another R5000 each; we didn't go crazy with our request – all we asked for was R15 000, and when they heard that, they threatened that they would use the Under-23 side instead. Eventually they agreed to give us R20 000 each when all we wanted was R15 000."

The game was a highly competitive one and we lost 2–1 with a dubious call against us. Although there was a hand-ball incident outside the area, the referee awarded a penalty against us, when everyone but him saw exactly where it had taken place.

When we signed out of the hotel the following day, I was presented with a massive bill for the golf carts. I wasn't in a very happy mood and simply passed the invoice on to our team manager

Glyn Binkin and headed for the bus. To this day, I have no idea who addressed the matter.

With this said and done, however, this side was still special and could play anywhere in the world. Unfortunately, it went into decline after embarking on that campaign to play the best 10 teams in the world. Bafana had qualified for the World Cup but I thought our best preparation would be to play against strong opposition rather than go into the competition under prepared. This was the country's first-ever World Cup appearance and we wanted to make a statement. Our opposition included the likes of Brazil (twice), France and England (away), Germany and Australia (home and away), Holland (home) and Argentina and Czech Republic (away).

In retrospect, perhaps our failure was because the quality of the opposition might have been a tad too strong.

It was during our qualification for the World Cup that I was faced with a huge decision – possibly the biggest I had ever had to make.

I remember watching Neil Tovey in the twilight of his international career, when other good players were catching up to him. I started having doubts as to whether he would be first choice in the side; were Mark Fish and Lucas Radebe not a better combination?

When we went to Togo for a World Cup qualifier, I decided to make my choice; I called a meeting of my technical team and briefed them on my decision to release one of the great sons of South African sport. Francois Pienaar, Hansie Cronjé and Neil Tovey were, at the time, sporting ambassadors of Nelson Mandela, and I had chosen to replace a tough man, Neil 'Mkoko' Tovey, albeit with another icon, Lucas 'Rhoo' Radebe.

Although Neil was no longer the captain, he did go to the World Cup with Bafana Bafana when Philippe Troussier took over from Jomo Sono, who had led them to the final of the 1998 Africa Cup of Nations, but could not convince SAFA to make his temporary appointment a permanent one.

I don't know that I would have made any improvement on being knocked out of the group stages at the World Cup; neither would Jomo.

Philippe Troussier was the wrong guy at the wrong time. Not that he wasn't a good coach, but his reaction to failure was terrible. If the side lost because of a dead-ball situation, at the next training session he would get 10 balls, form a wall and run up and drive the ball into the players' faces. If they flinched, then the training session would continue in much the same way.

He wasn't the nicest guy in the world either and sent two players back from the first World Cup. Funnily enough, Mark Fish was out at the same party that caused all the trouble, but he remained with the team because Troussier believed he needed Mark too much to send home.

The Confederations Cup marked the sad ending of my time with Bafana Bafana.

Perhaps the Benedict McCarthy scenario was a sign of impending disaster that would signal my exit as national coach.

In my mind, I was building the team that was most likely to represent Bafana at the World Cup in France, with a strike force comprising Philemon Masinga, Shaun Bartlett and Mark Williams.

But appearing on the horizon was a hugely talented new kid on the block, Benni McCarthy, who would most likely replace Daniel Mudau. At the back, Quinton Fortune of Manchester United fame was also knocking at the door. Left-footed, he offered good balance.

I invited the pair to play against France in a friendly match, with Benni coming on late in the game and immediately comfortable playing at international level. Both thanked me for the opportunity I had given them and they appeared to have made an impact: they were then welcomed into the squad.

However, both players' agents had other ideas.

A mouth-watering fixture – a return match against Brazil – was being arranged by SAFA and I invited the two players because this represented an opportunity to showcase them both at home.

Brazil were visiting South Africa for the final warm-up match before the Confederations Cup and this would be the ideal time for Benni to show his abilities against top-class opposition. We gave him the opportunity to play, but he never pitched. His agent had decided to turn the offer down.

I called the digs where he was staying, but the woman in charge was adamant that Benni was not there. I continued to try to reach him, but without success; clearly there was something at play here. Looking back, Benni, his agent and quite possibly a third individual took away the opportunity to assemble what might have been the best Bafana team ever.

By this point in my coaching career, I think I'd had enough. Irritating but unsettling doubts were starting to creep in. One issue was players not being paid on time – a catastrophe that could have a huge influence on results. The other was the players striking in England.

But there was one last assignment: the Confederations Cup. Replacing the King Fahd Cup in 1997, it was the first competition to feature representatives from all of the FIFA confederations.

Group A consisted of Brazil (1994 FIFA World Cup winners) who beat Australia 6–0 in the final, Australia (1996 OFC Nations Cup winners), Saudi Arabia (hosts and 1996 AFC Asian Cup winners) and Mexico (1996 CONCACAF Gold Cup winners), while Group B featured Uruguay (1995 Copa América winners), South Africa (1996 Africa Cup of Nations winners), Czech Republic (UEFA Euro 1996 runners-up) and United Arab Emirates (1996 AFC Asian Cup runners-up).

We got a helluva result in our first match for the Confederations Cup, drawing 2–2 with the Czech Republic who were fourth in the world in the FIFA rankings at the time. So it was that I was having supper at the hotel that evening when the SAFA chairman Molefi Oliphant and Irvin Khoza came into the restaurant, and proceeded right past me without so much as an acknowledgement. I couldn't believe what had just happened.

The same behaviour repeated itself two days later after we lost 1–0 to the United Arab Emirates.

I thought that the best thing would be to confront them, so I did. They promptly turned around and claimed that the fans back home in South Africa were stoning the players' houses, disgusted at our play and demanding changes.

My response was that if I was the catalyst for bad things then we needed to have a meeting. When we did meet, Irvin promised that my contract would be honoured if I resigned, which SAFA did, paying me on a regular basis. I have no qualms with that.

We went on to lose 4–3 to Uruguay in our final match – hardly a disgrace, but by then there was no turning back.

I think, in retrospect, I was a coward because I let those players down. I believe they would have had a great World Cup if we had all remained together. Perhaps no more successful than where they ended up, but certainly a lot happier. South Africa was at the World Cup for the first time; we had qualified the right way – there was no back-door entry – but I still feel that I let them down. It was a poor decision to make because, if I had stuck with them, SAFA would never have got rid of me; people wouldn't have allowed it.

How sad that it didn't work out.

But there was one more incident that left a sour taste in my mouth.

After I had gone in to negotiate the terms of the termination of my contract, Glyn Binkin went in to speak about his future with the national team. He had played a huge role in Bafana's success at the Africa Cup of Nations and was superb in how he looked after the players during the tournament.

With Glyn's meeting finished, he came directly to me. There was a knock on the door of my hotel room and there he stood, sobbing. He was so upset: SAFA were not going to renew his contract. I couldn't believe it so I rushed outside to Irvin Khoza who was in his car, leaving the hotel. I asked what was happening, he refused to talk but assured me we'd chat another time. When we did in fact do so a couple of days later, he confirmed that they no longer wanted Glyn, probably because he was too close to the players. So they booted him out. I was appalled.

Outside of Butch Webster, I know Glyn was the best team manager I've ever worked with, an absolute pillar of strength.

*Clive coaching Wits University in 2013 – the only Gauteng-based team
he has coached during his career.*

TWENTY

The Way Forward

I n 1996 South Africa were the champions of Africa and ranked 16th in FIFA's world rankings. A year later we qualified for our first World Cup. The groundwork had been done to allow the country to grow into an international powerhouse on the continent and beyond.

But 22 years later we have yet to repeat the 1996 heroics and we languish in 78th position in the world rankings. Why have we not progressed from that glorious day in 1996 when we were crowned African champions?

Is it because SAFA hired inferior coaches after I left?

Carlos Queiroz and Carlos Alberto Parreira were enticed to coach Bafana Bafana but neither of their respective teams achieved success even though they are some of the most qualified and successful coaches in football.

Were the players who came after the likes of Khumalo, Masinga and Fish lesser talents? I'm sure observers of the on-field exploits of Aaron Mokoena, Quinton Fortune and Steven Pienaar would argue against that.

Was it that we played the Africa Cup of Nations 1996 on home soil so had an unfair advantage? And yet we hosted the World Cup in 2010 and became the first home nation not to advance beyond the group stage. In 2013 we hosted the Africa Cup of Nations and lost in the quarterfinals.

Was it because our local league was in better shape in 1996 than it was in 2016? The local Premiership was ranked in the top 15 leagues in the world in terms of broadcast and sponsorship value. We have some of the most professionally run clubs in Africa in the form of Kaizer Chiefs, Orlando Pirates and Mamelodi Sundowns.

So what is the problem? Could it be the administrators, the SAFA structures that have governed our national game since 1992? Coaches get fired and players are dropped and those same administrators keep their jobs. There is no logic to the working lifespan of the administrators who run not only football but sport in general, in South Africa.

Had a company performed as badly as Bafana has over the past 22 years, the shareholders would have sacked the CEO and his management team a long time ago. So I point a finger at SAFA not because I'm bitter that they 'sacked me' in 1997, but because they have not built on our legacy.

Many detractors may think that I – or any of the '96 players – welcome Bafana Bafana's continued failings because it enhances our reputations. But that's simply not true. We want our legacies to be laid to rest, replaced by something that is an improvement. We want to walk down the street and have a fan say: "You guys were great in 1996 but can you compare yourself to this Bafana team who won the 2021 AFCON title and reached the quarterfinals of the World Cup in Qatar?"

We wanted those glory days to act as a catalyst for the creation of the powerhouse that South African football should be. We wanted to take credit for birthing the footballing giant we are capable of becoming.

So what is the solution?

Senegal's fans decided to use their democratic right to force the removal of the Senegalese administrators after their team lost out on qualification for the 2010 World Cup after drawing 1–1 with lowly Gambia. Since then, Senegal have become one of Africa's best teams, sporting the likes of Sadio Mané and company, and competing in Russia in 2018. At the time of writing this book, they were in 27th position on the FIFA rankings, 50 places above South Africa.

We, the collective body of football in the country – players, fans, officials – need to make changes in running our football and it starts at the top. SAFA needs an overhaul to make sure young professional blood is brought in to administer the game in all its facets: marketing, sponsorship, media, team structure and most importantly development.

Development is the word everyone reaches for when searching for a solution to our lack of footballing prowess. But what is development? Take raw teen talent from the dusty townships and house it in professional academies in up-market suburbs and it will evolve into professional world-class talent? I wish it were that easy; if it were, the world's most populous nations would be unbeatable, but China, India, America don't have any World Cup titles to their credit.

You can't nurture talent by taking that talent out of its environment – you have to go into that environment and put structures in place there to develop the talent where it is found. Football is not just about your physical prowess; it is also about mental ability and too often players can't cope with new environments thrust upon them.

The common denominator for all our youngsters in the country is their enrolment in school structures and I believe development has to take place at school level. The facilities are there; they might vary in terms of standards, but the structure is there. The participation is there, but there needs to be a plan that allows those kids access to standard facilities and coaching know-how to ensure they can progress.

I believe the biggest blight on SAFA's development record has been the lack of establishing 'footballing' high schools. Take the players who have represented South African rugby since we won the World Cup in 1995 and 50 per cent of the players would have come from the top 20 rugby schools in the country, be it Grey College, Paarl Gym or King Edward. The same applies to cricket, but where are these schools in terms of acting as development hubs for football?

How have rugby and cricket managed, in partnership with the school structure, to ensure a steady flow of talent from their classrooms? My former school, Glenwood in Durban, have through their excellent structures produced the likes of Warren Whiteley (Springbok) and Andile Phehlukwayo (Proteas) in recent years but why are there no players from Glenwood in the Bafana squad?

Football is by far the biggest, most supported, most funded sport in South Africa, dwarfing rugby and cricket. Orlando Pirates' yearly sponsorship betters any deal the national teams of cricket and rugby enjoy. So the money is there, the structures are there, the facilities are there, the talent is there but the leadership to steer it effectively is not.

As our country enjoys the changing of the guard at political level I hope those winds of change blow firmly through SAFA House.

I have also highlighted that the decay of the amateur football structures is a major cause for the demise of our football. In the 1970s and '80s the amateur football scene was healthy and thriving. In Durban, clubs such as Ramblers, Wanderers, Stella, Fynnlands, Virginia and Westville had juniors and seniors, from Under-8s to adults, playing on Friday nights and Saturday and Sunday afternoons.

Each club had up to 12 Under-8 teams. This was not uncommon in all the amateur setups. Each team played in their respective leagues on a regular basis and a very high standard of football was being achieved.

The grounds were well kept, cut and marked. As many as two to three thousand might have watched a local derby at any given time. This situation was echoed throughout the country.

We now have many sports grounds standing empty, derelict and completely vandalised. They are municipal property and it is well nigh impossible to reach an amicable arrangement with regard to utilising the space to benefit the amateur footballing community, of all ages and races.

The opportunity to integrate all young players keen to be trained and developed into cohesive and productive leagues is being wasted. There seems to be an apathy and disinterest hampering any progress that might be possible.

The only way that South Africa can realise its full potential on the international football stage is when we have established fully equipped academies, with respected technical and coaching staff. It is imperative to recognise talent, create the environment to allow its growth, and produce players to feed the professional leagues and national teams.

It will take dedication, hard work and absolute commitment to make this vision a reality. We need to restore national pride in South African football.

Clive doing what he loves most, training and nurturing young talent and hopefully the next generation of Bafana Bafana stars.

TWENTY-ONE

In Closing

"We played football like people want football to be played. If that's how I am remembered, then that's the greatest acknowledgement I could ever hope for."

– CLIVE BARKER

guess no life story is complete without voicing a few regrets. One was accepting such a low salary when I was asked to coach Bafana Bafana. The other is losing out on the chance to coach elsewhere. I would have loved to have the opportunity of coaching Chiefs or Pirates or Sundowns, the clubs with big money to spend, lots of support for the players and for the team itself.

At one stage, Saudi Arabia were talking about me and the team, which was something of an ego boost, affirmation that we were doing the right things and people were noticing. The Chinese national football hierarchy came across to meet me at the Protea Hotel in Umhlanga in an attempt to lure me over there, but I was so naïve about matters like this. They wanted an answer from me about who I wanted in my support, medical and technical team right away. The deal was that they would pay me all the money and I would then pay my staff. I think if I'd been able to give them an answer there and then, I would more than likely have coached the

Chinese national team.

We had negotiated a R100 000 bonus if we won the Africa Cup of Nations. We did win; we also won the Four Nations tournament three times and qualified for the World Cup in France. When Carlos Parreira coached Bafana, he was paid R1.7 million a month. That was to win nothing and qualify for nothing.

Somehow I got it all wrong.

The three big sports in South Africa are cricket, rugby and football, and while the cricketers weren't achieving on a grand scale, like a World Cup, I knew the pressure that would be on us the following year when Joel Stransky's drop goal at the 1995 Rugby World Cup Final went through. The coach of the Springboks was Kitch Christie and the captain Francois Pienaar. Bob Woolmer and Hansie Cronjé headed the Proteas and Neil Tovey and I represented Bafana Bafana. No black faces.

I think that drove away SAFA's support for me. I don't think there was any conniving behind the scenes, but I do think they would have preferred a black person at that stage and I could understand that – it made complete sense. Jomo Sono succeeded me and took Bafana to the final of the 1998 AFCON (losing to Egypt) before SAFA did a complete about turn and appointed a foreign (white) coach, Philippe Troussier, and that made no sense.

So, while SAFA never said anything about the racial make-up of the team, I sensed there was a problem and quit when I should have stayed and have taken them to the World Cup; I regret not having had that opportunity. I was a coward not to stand by the players.

Although people have spoken of me as a strong motivator, I'd hate to think that they see me as a monkey jumping up and down, motivating players. If that's how people think I got results, they're completely wrong.

The Bafana side I took over had lost a number of games by big margins so it took more than just motivation to turn the results around. There were other technical aspects that we needed to work on and get right; picking players to blend together was a big factor in our success.

Another significant factor was man management. I would get my team fit, healthy and wanting to play rather than worrying about the opposition. People would ask if I had videos of our opponents' previous matches and I kept saying that if my side didn't play to their potential then they certainly wouldn't beat anyone, regardless of whether we had researched them or not.

Carl Peters provides an outsider's perspective, having written about Bafana in his capacity as newspaper journalist and someone who spent a lot of time analysing the team.

Many people shared the view that Clive had become too loyal to his team, which was being referred to as Barker's Babes, that he didn't bring fresh faces into the team soon enough. The players he had were top names, still legends of South African football, but perhaps he should have refreshed the team sooner. Also, the matches became tougher because we were playing more European teams in the build-up to the World Cup in France. Those losses went against his name, together with the results in the Confederations Cup and, even though it was part of a building programme, saw the end of him.

The crowds love him, the people of the country love him, but he tends to rile the administrators because he never listens to anything they say, which irks them. Towards the end of his tenure as national coach, there was a growing sense of resentment because he was seen by some as the only one taking credit for Bafana Bafana's successes. There were a lot of people in the background who were upset and who resented the Barker's Babes nickname.

– Carl Peters

When Bafana first started out – and they don't like the reference – they were called the Four-by-Fours. That Four-by-Four team included the likes of Neil Tovey, Mark Fish and Lucas Radebe, so these big stars for Bafana also got thumped. But the greatest satisfaction I gained was the improvement in those same players and how much better they played in time. Many of them gravitated overseas and played with distinction in Europe and elsewhere. Lucas Radebe and Philemon Masinga at Leeds, Doctor Khumalo in America, Shoes Moshoeu in Turkey and Eric Tinkler in Portugal. So they certainly didn't go out and perform for Bafana simply making up the numbers; they improved and that improvement was what I gained the most enjoyment and satisfaction from.

I saw them go from nobodies to somebodies and playing the 10 best teams in the world, most of them home as well as away. They were able to take on the finest sides and play with distinction; I never felt that we would ever get a thumping. The only time I doubted the team's ability and took no responsibility for that was playing against Germany away, when Chiefs, Pirates, Manning Rangers and Sundowns played in the semifinals of a cup competition and wouldn't allow their players to represent their country. Outside of that 3–0 loss to Germany, the results were fabulous and always fairly evenly matched against the big teams.

In our first match against Brazil, you looked up and there was Cafu and Rivaldo and Bebeto, fantastic players representing a world champion team. We ran them close – very, very close. Outside of our semifinal performance against Ghana in the 1996 Africa Cup of Nations, this performance was up there with the best.

Representing the sports apparel company Puma at a five-a-side tournament in Austria was also an occasion when I really felt the acknowledgement of what I had achieved with Bafana Bafana. Richard Michael had joined Pumas and between the two of us we selected an Under-13 South African Puma XI. At the draw for the cup competition, as I walked past the Brazilian players, they all stood up and mimicked my aeroplane victory run; for me, that was the best recognition I ever received. A lot of people have said to me that they still talk about that game over in Brazil. I'm delighted that we made such an impression on them.

Bafana's strengths were the desire to win and to be someone. The Madiba influence at the Africa Cup of Nations in 1996 was a considerable factor too. Consistent selection gave the players confidence in themselves; they trusted each other on the field and loved each other off it. This led to consistency in play and the resulting success.

All of us may have paid the price in the end. We kept getting results and we would test the boundaries further and further, against opposition teams such as England, France, Czech Republic, Brazil and Germany.

The players loved one another and each other's company – they loved the whole environment; we never had to invite them a second time to come and play. They would show absolutely no hesitation in returning. The club-versus-country debate was never an issue for us. They just loved being together, the singalongs on the bus, the competitions. Each player had a personality and that made them unique.

An often-asked question of me is to identify which players I would turn to in a crisis. Sugar Ray Xulu would be the one from the 1970s while Calvin Petersen and Professor Ngubane were invaluable during the 1980s. In the 1990s, John 'Shoes' Moshoeu, Doctor Khumalo, Neil Tovey and Lucas Radebe were pillars of strength.

But for setting up chances in a game, the best player I have ever worked with is the incomparable Doctor Khumalo. There is a hit song by Tina Turner – 'Simply the Best'.

That is Doctor Khumalo.

"Clive was a real father figure to all the team members," says Doc. "He instilled a lot of confidence in many players like myself and the late Shoes. His strength was getting the best out of an individual and he inspired me by having so much confidence in me. He was always convincing me that I was one of the individuals who could turn around the game situations."

Some people say that Clive is just a motivator, but motivation doesn't win trophies or tournaments like the Africa Cup of Nations. What about the other top coaches, and there have been many? They haven't been able to win the AFCON. Clive was special. They talk about José Mourinho as "the special one", but Clive was special. Clive had the feel for the game and the understanding of players' personalities and abilities. He got the best out of them.

He was a damn good coach and an amazing person. There's something about him, many people communicate but don't connect, but he connected with the players. He loved his players, he always treated them as something special, he'd do anything for them. We'd arrive in the changing room before a game and each of us find our kit neatly packed in a bag, with our name on, we were made to feel valued.

He was a real player's coach – you want to play for a coach like that. He was like a father to us; he would do anything for a player, but don't stab him in the back, because then you'll be in serious trouble. He could get the best out of any player; he made you believe you were as good as he was telling you that you were.

– Calvin Petersen

Clive had no peer as football coach. It was testament to his calm temperament that he never panicked. He could handle any situation, although there would be times when the vein in his neck would stand out and we knew the pressure cooker was threatening to blow.

His personality, his demeanour was so good for the game. He could motivate players like no one else; he knew when to hit them hard, when to be soft on them. People would die for Clive. Whether he is coaching a 10-year-old kid or a multimillionaire player, he has the same passion, the same enthusiasm and the same heart. His glass-half-full attitude has made him the person he is today. He's a true legend – there's no other description for him. The only tragedy was that he was not able to continue with Bafana Bafana in France.

– Butch Webster

When we stayed at the Sunnyside Hotel during the Africa Cup of Nations, Clive gave us plenty of time off, and although we had guys in our team who might push the boundaries, he would never send security to check up on us. He was very approachable; you could knock on his door and he'd open it and invite you in and talk to you. And he would listen, really listen to you so that when you had had your say, you would come out of his hotel room satisfied that your concerns had been taken to heart.

Clive was a real one-of-a-kind coach, I don't think we'll have another coach like him. If you ask any of those players from the 1996 Bafana team who the best coach they've ever played under, and I'm taking the AFCON success out of the picture, they'll all say Clive was.

There have been many footballing stars, but few make their name as a coach; Clive is one of them. In fact, as a coach, he is legendary and being coached by Clive was a great personal honour.

Since 1996 when we won the Africa Cup of Nations, we've had 15 coaches probably, something like 700 players and Bafana have gone from number 16 in the world to 70 or 80. The money has gone from zero then to hundreds of millions of rands now. Seen in that context, Clive did an unbelievable job given what he had at his disposal at the time.

– Glyn Binkin

You could see that the 1996 Bafana team was well prepared; it was a happy team, a contented group of players. To win the Africa Cup of Nations takes science, physical and mental preparation, talent and a generation of players who have been playing together for some time. It's not a flash in the pan to win the Africa Cup of Nations; you need everyone pulling in the same direction and a coach who knows how to deploy his men.

You can have a good team, but you have to treat this like a chess game, each piece with its own strengths and abilities.

And if your players don't sweat blood, they're not going to end up as champions of Africa. Clive earned a lot of respect as a coach because of what he was able to get out of his players. The players he coached still speak about him fondly. I have great respect for Clive because of the good things he did and the team he put together.

– Kalusha Bwalya

You can have all the stars, all the big names, but to get them to play together as a team is completely different and takes a special kind of talent, a special kind of person. That was Clive; his great achievement was getting all the characters and personalities focused on one goal.

– Lucas Radebe

The fact that we had the full support of the South African nation for the Africa Cup of Nations tournament was something very special that will live in my memory forever.

The tournament was very long but because of the spirit and camaraderie in camp, it seemed to flash by very quickly. The fact that Clive allowed us to go and celebrate the victories after the game and be with our families and be with the fans made the whole experience even more special and easy to endure. Sitting back now and looking at what we achieved as a team makes one think about the pressure we were under as a team, yet at no stage did any of us feel that pressure and credit must go to Clive for achieving that.

– Eric Tinkler

If you look back at our success, we were fortunate to have an unbelievable team and you need a coach to select the right players and once we had that, after we won that first Africa Cup of Nations match, we realised that we had a chance to win the tournament. He had the right people around him and was the right person you need to be at international level.

Clive should never have resigned as national coach; I

believe he did it before he would have been bulleted. But at the 1997 Confederations Cup, we drew 2-2 with Czech Republic who had lost in the final at Euro '96 and were a great team and we lost to Uruguay 4-3 in our final match. We were playing unbelievable football against top teams (South Africa won the Fair Play Award).

He shouldn't have done it, it was a very big mistake. Whatever information SAFA had, Clive had definitely not lost the team. He had done his job, won the Africa Cup of Nations and we'd qualified for the 1998 Soccer World Cup; there must have been someone with a hidden agenda to get rid of him. It may have been a rash decision, but since then, South African football has not tasted the successes we had under him.

– Mark Fish

He knew when to step in and be forceful and when it was time to bring humour into the session. He knew how to wind players up; it would be fiercely contested, but in a good way, and that's sadly missing in today's coaching. There is this rigorous mentality, no light-heartedness comes into it, but you need balance and you need to know how to balance being focused, strict and forceful, and when to be light-hearted. Clive had that knack.

His area of expertise, his forte, in match situations can't be understated. He knew how he wanted the game played, he knew what and who he wanted in the core of his team and where he could have the luxury of playing X-factor players like a Doctor Khumalo or a Lawrence Chelin and you'll find that in all his teams.

Coaching isn't only about training. You spend loads of time with the coach: travelling, analysing, away on trips, staying in hotels. It was fun, everywhere we went was fun; but there was always focus and he knew how to rein in a player when it was getting too much fun. A people's coach, a player's coach.

Sometimes that was to his detriment; there were times when people didn't take his knowledge of the game that seriously – they saw him more as a motivational coach rather than someone who could read the game. You can't win the Africa Cup of Nations or league championships or trophies if you haven't read the game situation for a particular match because you can plan and prepare as much as you like, but when in the game situation, it takes a different dimension to coaching. You need to know what your team is capable of doing and sum up the opposition very quickly. That wasn't an attribute people spoke about with reference to Clive, but having come through his coaching, I know he was very knowledgeable in that area of the game.

I can't thank Clive enough for being part of the success. He played a significant role in my life; our paths have crossed numerous times over the years. But I think he made a big mistake after 1996 when he didn't take up the job opportunities he was offered. He's a sentimental person; sometimes you need to be ruthless. Perhaps he's been too loyal when people have kicked him in the butt. But you can't deny that he has lived by his principles.

– Neil Tovey

Common sense and a desire to overcome irrational laws was the very reason why the apartheid government would never win in the end. Many people fought from inside this country, and the likes of Irvin Khoza and Kaizer Motaung never sold their souls. I was delighted to be involved in the struggle in some way.

When people ask me what the pinnacle of my career was, I could reflect fondly on the 1996 Africa Cup of Nations, qualifying for the World Cup in France in 1998, winning the Four Nations three times, three League titles or nine national Cup Finals. But above all was the inauguration of a man I was honoured to meet a number of times, Nelson Mandela.

On that day as he was sworn in as South Africa's first democratic president, he came to watch us play Zambia. The vibe was electric and 60 000 cheering supporters made sure they were there to celebrate with him.

At the end of the Africa Cup of Nations Final, when the whistle blew, I saw FW de Klerk, King Goodwill Zwelithini and Nelson Mandela all walking across the pitch together, holding hands, and for the first time, I thought that South Africa really was united.

That we really had a chance. I still believe this to be true.

Appendix A

Coaching History – South African Professional
Club Football

1974–1976
Head Coach: AmaZulu Football Club
Honours:
1974 South African Cup Runners-up (versus Orlando Pirates –
Mainstay Cup Final)
1976 South African Cup Runners-up (versus Kaizer Chiefs)

1976
Head Coach: Pinetown Celtic
Honours:
1976 National League Second Division Champions

1977–1980

Head Coach: Juventus Football Club

Honours:

1977 1st Division Winners

1978 Natal League Winners

1980 Premier Amateur League Winners

1981–1984

Head Coach: Durban City Football Club

Honours:

1982 South African League Champions

1983 South African League Champions

1984 South African Cup Runners-up (versus Kaizer Chiefs)

1984–1985

Head Coach: Durban Bush Bucks Football Club

Honours:

1984 South African Cup Runners-up

1985 South African League Champions

1985 South African League Cup Runners-up

1985–1987, 1992–1993 and 1997–1999

Head Coach: AmaZulu Football Club

Honours:

1986 South African League 3rd Place

1987 South African League Runners-up

1992 South African League Cup Champions (versus Kaizer Chiefs, Winners 3–1)

2000–2001

Head Coach: Santos Football Club

Honours:

2001 South African Cup Champions (FNB Cup Final versus Mamelodi Sundowns, Winners 1–0)

2001–2003
Head Coach: Manning Rangers Football Club

2003
Head Coach: Maritzburg United

2004
Head Coach: Zulu Royals

2005
Head Coach: Manning Rangers

2005
Head Coach: Santos Cape Town

2006
Head Coach: Bush Bucks

2006
Head Coach: AmaZulu

2007–2009
Head Coach: AmaZulu

2013
Head Coach: Bidvest Wits

2013–2015
Head Coach: Black Aces

2015–2016
Head Coach: Maritzburg United

Appendix B

Coaching History – South African Senior National Team

8 May 1994 – 17 December 1997
Record as Coach of National Team
Played: 43
Won: 22
Drew: 9
Lost: 12
Goals for: 57
Goals against: 38

Honours:
1994 Four Nations Cup Winner
1995 Four Nations Cup Winner
1996 Four Nations Cup Winner
1996 Africa Nations Cup Champions
1997 Qualified South Africa for 1998 World Cup

Match-by-match Statistics

1994-05-08:	SA 1 Zimbabwe 0, Friendly (H)
1994-05-10:	SA 2 Zambia 1, Friendly (H)
1994-06-08:	SA 0 Australia 1, Friendly (A)
1994-06-12:	SA 0 Australia 1, Friendly (A)
1994-09-04:	SA 1 Madagascar 0, ACN Qualifier (A)
1994-10-15:	SA 1 Mauritius 0, ACN Qualifier (H)
1994-11-13:	SA 1 Zambia 1, ACN Qualifier (A)
1994-11-26:	SA 2 Ghana 1, Four Nations Cup (H)
1994-11-30:	SA 0 Cote d'Ivoire 0, Four Nations Cup (H)
1994-12-03:	SA 1 Cameroon 1, Four Nations Cup (H)
1995-04-26:	SA 3 Lesotho 0, Friendly (A)
1995-05-13:	SA 1 Argentina 1, Friendly (H)
1995-09-30:	SA 3 Mozambique 2, Friendly (H)
1995-11-22:	SA 2 Zambia 2, Four Nations Cup (H)
1995-11-24:	SA 2 Egypt 0, Four Nations Cup (H)
1995-11-26:	SA 2 Zimbabwe 0, Four Nations Cup (H)
1995-12-15:	SA 0 Germany 0, Friendly (H)
1996-01-13:	SA 3 Cameroon 0, ACN Finals (H)
1996-01-20:	SA 1 Angola 0, ACN Finals (H)
1996-01-24:	SA 0 Egypt 1, ACN Finals (H)
1996-01-27:	SA 2 Algeria 1, ACN Quarterfinal (H)
1996-01-31:	SA 3 Ghana 0, ACN Semifinal (H)
1996-02-03:	SA 2 Tunisia 0, ACN Final (H)
1996-04-24:	SA 2 Brazil 3, Friendly (H)
1996-06-01:	SA 1 Malawi 0, World Cup Qualifier (A)
1996-06-15:	SA 3 Malawi 0, World Cup Qualifier (H)
1996-09-14:	SA 1 Kenya 0, Four Nations Cup (H)
1996-09-18:	SA 2 Australia 0, Four Nations Cup (H)
1996-09-21:	SA 0 Ghana 0, Four Nations Cup (H)
1996-11-09:	SA 1 Zaire 0, World Cup Qualifier (H)
1997-01-11:	SA 0 Zambia 0, World Cup Qualifier (A)
1997-04-06:	SA 0 Congo 2, World Cup Qualifier (A)
1997-04-27:	SA 2 Zaire 1, World Cup Qualifier (A)
1997-05-24:	SA 1 England 2, Friendly (A)
1997-06-04:	SA 0 The Netherlands 2, Friendly (H)

1997-06-08:   SA 3 Zambia 0, World Cup Qualifier (H)

1997-08-16:   SA 1 Congo 0, World Cup Qualifier (H)

1997-10-11:   SA 0 France 1, Friendly (A)

1997-11-15:   SA 0 Germany 3, Friendly (A)

1997-12-07:   SA 1 Brazil 2, Friendly (H)

1997-12-13:   SA 2 Czech Republic 2, Confederations Cup (A)

1997-12-15:   SA 0 United Arab Emirates 1, Confederations Cup (A)

1997-12-17:   SA 3 Uruguay 4, Confederations Cup (A)

Acknowledgements

I HAVE A DEBT OF GRATITUDE TO those good friends, acquaintances and family members who have been so loyal and supportive and who have given me sensible advice over the years.

I will probably leave some people out, and I beg their forgiveness.

I thank Yvonne, my wife, whom I married in 1968, for always being there for me and knowing how to get the best out of me. She is discerning and, with her positive attitude, has always had the ability to turn bad situations into good.

She did not attend many matches over the years but would always show a keen interest in the results and not be shy about offering advice and comment on the teams' and individual player's performances. I guess, with her international experience as a ballet teacher and examiner for the Cecchetti Society and KZN Dance Academy, she understands the discipline required in training and shepherding players into a cohesive and successful team.

I admire both my sons' achievements in their chosen careers and my heart swells with pride when I think of their families and how they have impacted on Yvonne and my life.

John is a respected movie producer, director and scriptwriter, and his wife Marilyn runs a well-established nursery school. They have three beautiful sons: Garcia, Caleb and Eli.

Gavin has a successful sports media business and his wife Liza a confectionary business. They have two lovely sons: Byron and Luca.

My brother-in-law Carl, a costume and dress designer, is an important part of the family unit and has always been there for us all, especially when I travelled. I have a sister Penny and two deceased brothers, Laurie and Arthur, who played a role in defining my way forward in football. To my nephew Steve Barker who was a really top player (Wits University) and went on to coach at the highest level (University of Pretoria and AmaZulu) in this country.

My national and international coaching career has taken a huge toll on my family and I am so grateful that they have embraced the ups and downs and helped me remain focused and grounded.

Many business colleagues have become true friends and have propped me up along the way. It is difficult to express the sincere gratitude I feel for Param Joseph, especially during my recent ill-health; he was much like Afzal Kahn – very knowledgeable about football in South Africa – and we would spend many hours discussing the players we would love to attract to Manning Rangers where he was a director. Graham O'Connor helped to keep football alive in KZN by influencing SPAR South Africa to sponsor AmaZulu. Les Pillay, from Build-It, has involved me in the Under-13 national tournaments and Coach-the-Coaches events. Wayne Amos was instrumental in compiling the manuals for the Coach-the-Coaches courses.

To all the directors, chairmen, managers and coaching staff with whom I have worked, I offer my deepest appreciation for the invaluable assistance and counsel given to me in this most demanding team sport.

My grateful thanks to Philani Mabaso, who I have enjoyed working with since our AmaZulu days together. As someone who always showed great initiative, once again his valuable contribution, this time in helping this book come to fruition, is hugely appreciated.

I would also like to extend my appreciation to Deirdre Mullan who performed the role of project manager with distinction.

Without the interest and involvement of Rajendran Reddy of KZN Oil, the concept of this book would have remained just a dream.

To Michael Marnewick, one of the most accommodating, patient and long-suffering people I have worked with: a humble and inadequate thank you.

I need to also acknowledge the time and input for this book received from my wonderful sons John and Gavin and lastly my wife Yvonne, for making sense of my rambling notes.

Index